"This wonderful study on the blessings given by Israel upon his twelve sons shows us how we can proactively possess the opportunities of the blessings and find redemption for our failures. And it gives us warning of errors that rob us of the opportunities that blessing affords. Let us possess our blessings."

Dr. Roger Houtsma, Roger Houtsma World Outreach

"In this book, Pastor Paul has blended together history and theology with his personal journey in ministry, walking with God by faith. His insights, revelation and application of Scripture regarding the blessings pronounced on the twelve tribes will enrich, inspire and invigorate the believer's faith in God and His Word. A fascinating read."

Rev. Giuloio Lorefice Gabeli, national director,
Canada Celebrates Israel Network; author,
Grafted In: A Jewish-Christian Perspective

"Paul Thangiah is an anointed apostolic minister. *Receiving the 12 Blessings of Israel* is a unique and compelling presentation resulting from Pastor Paul's personal study of Scripture. This book will provoke thought and study and will increase faith to allow God to fulfill His pronounced blessings."

David L. Grant, co-founder and director, Project Rescue

RECEIVING THE 12 BLESSINGS OF ISRAEL

RECEIVING THE 12 BLESSINGS OF ISRAEL

How *God's Promises* TO HIS PEOPLE APPLY TO *Your Life* TODAY

PAUL THANGIAH

Chosen

a division of Baker Publishing Group
Minneapolis, Minnesota

Published by Chosen Books
11400 Hampshire Avenue South
Bloomington, Minnesota 55438
www.chosenbooks.com

Chosen Books is a division of
Baker Publishing Group, Grand Rapids, Michigan

Printed in the United States of America

Library of Congress Control Number: 2016938473

ISBN 978-0-8007-9807-9

Cover design by Rob Williams, InsideOutCreativeArts

16 17 18 19 20 21 22   7 6 5 4 3 2 1

Dedicated to:

MY DEAR FATHER,
the late Reverend A. R. Thangiah,
whose prayers and blessings on my life
are the reasons for the fruit in my ministry.

And to:

THE PEOPLE OF INDIA,
that they may be saved and
enjoy the blessings of God.

My father served the Lord for over 45 years and pioneered many churches in Sri Lanka. He further served with the Assemblies of God in the city of Madurai, India, where he founded New Life Assembly, which at present has 132 branches—all of which are strongly grounded in God's Word and are growing rapidly.

His prayers are indeed being answered, and his blessings are indeed being multiplied!

Contents

Foreword

In his new book, the Reverend Paul Thangiah analyzes the twelve tribes of Israel under a magnifying lens, looking closely at every aspect of the blessings upon them. Very few books have been written with such detail and understanding of the twelve tribes and how the blessings that Jacob the patriarch and Moses the prophet pronounced over them have relevance to the individual tribes, the nation of Israel and the modern-day Christian.

Pastor Paul details the blessings with respect to the lives of the twelve sons of Jacob and the future generations to come in the line of the tribes. The tribes are well defined by their characteristic features as detailed by Jacob and Moses. These characteristics lay the foundation for the fulfillment of multiple prophecies, and these prophecies, in turn, are reflected in the lives of the chosen few who rise up from each tribe when the situation needs them.

I commend Pastor Paul for undertaking this wide-ranging study, which demonstrates the need for us as modern Christians to reflect upon the ideas he presents. His insights warn us about the consequences of sin and motivate us to live godly lives dedicated to Christ alone.

It is difficult to summarize the treasures of this book in a few sentences. The deep meditation of the Reverend Thangiah on these blessings is a blessing of its own. I believe that as you carefully study and understand the divine truths recorded in this book, they will enrich your life and help you in your Christian walk.

Dr. George O. Wood, general superintendent,
Assemblies of God U.S.A.;
chairman, World Assemblies of God Fellowship

Acknowledgments

Many people have walked alongside me in my journey thus far. I am grateful to God for my dear mother, Hester Thangiah, whose faith in the Lord amazes me. She always strengthens herself in the Lord and then becomes a great source of strength to us.

My dear wife, Sheba, has been supportive all through the years. My daughter, Grace, and her dynamic husband, Neal, are very helpful and reliable. Grace runs my office efficiently as my executive assistant and events coordinator. Neal gives me helpful ideas and suggestions with his creative mind. My son, Sammy, and his wonderful wife, Nicole, have strengthened my hands in the church ministry as well. Even as they focus on the youth, they are ready to take the church into the next level along with me. Their son Malachi James is a bundle of joy and delight. I believe he will become a powerful messenger of the Lord who will grab the enemy by his heel and destroy him. Josiah Paul, their second son and the newest addition to our family, may be small, but will surely put a thousand to flight even as he gains the support of Yahweh.

Many stalwarts of the faith have mentored and taught me along the way. I thank God for each of these people who contributed to making my foundation strong:

Dr. Roger Houtsma has coached me personally on many things during his crusades in India, especially on venturing into the faith arena and seeing God do the impossible.

The late Dr. Hobart Grazier from Valley Forge taught me about the epistles to the Romans and Galatians, and he imparted to me the importance of studying the Word of God and letting it speak into my situations.

Dr. John Higgins and Faith Higgins have demonstrated servant leadership through their humility and simplicity. Dr. Higgins made the theology classes I took interesting and captivating. He taught me what we believe in and also why we believe it. Now nothing can shake me.

The Reverend Paul and Julie Williams trusted in me when I started pioneering the church, and they supported me financially by paying the rent for the house in which I began the work.

Dr. Naomi Dowdy, an inspiring woman of God, spent years investing into my life and ministry teaching me the importance of the Care Cell Ministry, which eventually helped in the growth of the church.

The Reverend Vernon and Sarah Davis gave me great insight and advice when God miraculously gave us the land on which we constructed the church.

I am also grateful to the many people who have helped and encouraged me along the way:

A word of appreciation goes to my dear friend the Reverend David Daniels, who invested into my ministry by gifting us the fans to fit into the new church building.

I also appreciate Dr. David and Dr. Beth Grant, who have been a great encouragement to me all through the years.

I appreciate Dr. Dick Bernal, who has been a great inspiration to me with his desire to reach out to non-Christians even in the midst of severe opposition.

I appreciate the Reverend Mark Daniels and his wife, Cathy, and Dr. Ivan Satyavrata and his wife, Sheila, for always surrounding me with words of wisdom, concern and prayer.

A special thanks to my close friend Dr. Cedric D. LaBrooy and his precious wife, Malli, who pastor Clayton Assembly of God in Melbourne, Australia, for standing with me when I went through the most difficult phase in my life.

I would also like to express my sincere gratitude to Dr. D. Mohan, who has been my mentor, a constant strength and guide to me. I am also grateful to the late Dr. T. C. George, who was the district superintendent when I launched into the ministry. He displayed tremendous faith in me even when others did not, and he stood with me and encouraged me. I really thank God for his life.

I am indebted to Jane Campbell, editorial director of Chosen Books, along with her publishing colleagues at Baker Publishing Group, for taking me through the publishing process. I am so grateful for their sanction and the way they helped me through each stage of getting this book published.

A special thank-you to Trish Konieczny for her remarkable assistance in the process of editing.

I express my deep gratitude to Dr. George O. Wood, chairman of the World Assemblies of God Fellowship, for gladly being willing to write the foreword for this book.

I would like to thank my editorial team, Pastor Rebecca Jaichandran, Pastor Jonathan Joel, Pastor Rachel John, Neal and Grace Mickey, Pastor Roger Samuel Thangiah and Pastor John V. Thomas, who worked along with me day and night.

Words will not suffice to thank my dear brother, Dr. Dudley Thangiah, and his wife, Saro, who pastor New Life Assembly in Madurai, for always being there for me. I also thank my brothers-in-law, Dr. David Balasingh and the Reverend Jeyasingh Vallal, who take such great delight in serving the Lord, and my sisters, Ruth Balasingh and Shanthi Jeyasingh, for all their love and concern for me.

Last but not least, I thank God for my pastors and my church, Full Gospel Assembly of God, for believing in the vision God gave me and for strengthening my hands in the ministry. I pray God's abundant blessings on all of them!

Introduction

God Desires to Bless His Children

Every time I read the Bible for my own spiritual growth and come upon the blessings Jacob pronounced over his sons in Genesis 49 and the blessings Moses spoke over the twelve tribes in Deuteronomy 33, I find them unique and interesting. For several years I had been thinking about doing an in-depth study on these two passages, but I never really got around to it. In December 2014, however, God prompted me to do the study and preach a series on it in our church. That marked the beginning of a fascinating examination of these passages. It opened my eyes to see that what they taught is not confined just to the sons of Jacob or the tribes of Israel; it extends to God's sons and daughters everywhere, to all those who are part of His Kingdom.

I began preaching the sermons on "The 12 Blessings of Israel" to my congregation the very first Sunday of 2015. Every Sunday throughout the series, we experienced a powerful move of God and people were stirred, touched and revived. On the whole, the response was overwhelming. That is when God prompted me to take the study and publish it as this book.

My purpose in writing this book, *Receiving the 12 Blessings of Israel: How God's Promises to His People Apply to Your Life Today*, is to help every child of God realize that God desires to bless His children. In fact, when God created us He already pronounced blessings on every one of us. All we need to do is understand that the promises of God are true and that we can trust them. The very fact that the tribal blessings pronounced by both Jacob and Moses came to pass affirms this to us.

It is interesting to note that some of the tribes had a good start, while others started as sinful and hopeless failures. Nevertheless, as they turned to God and depended on Him they were transformed, and they were able to see the fulfillment of the blessings pronounced on them. This emphasizes the fact that no one can ever say that he or she is not blessed or that God is partial. God's blessings will be fulfilled in the lives of those who turn to Him.

I am positive that at some point, each of us will be able to identify with one or more of the tribes I talk about. We will find ourselves in a situation similar to a particular tribe and say, "Hey, I know what Judah must have felt!" Or we will say, "I'm just going through what Reuben went through."

The good news is that God has made available all twelve of the blessings I talk about in and through Christ, for there is no condemnation in Christ. No one should ever assume, however, that these blessings come automatically. Rather, we must seek God through prayer, intense Bible study, fellowship and service.

In other words, to receive the twelve blessings, we have to walk in fellowship with God and grow in maturity. We can claim the blessings of any tribe or all of the tribes on our lives, as long as we walk in repentance and dependence on Christ.

I trust this book will help you understand that God has pronounced blessings on you and that He has the power to fulfill them. No matter how sinful or hopeless you may be, if you are willing to repent and seek God, you can enjoy the twelve blessings. I am convinced that as you flip through the pages of this book, every bondage over your life will be broken and you will be blessed beyond measure. At the end of every chapter, we will pray together about just that. Receive your blessings!

Let's Pray Together

Dear God, we know that You are El Shaddai, the all-sufficient God. You are all we want . . . You are all we ever need! You have good plans for us. Your plans are to prosper us and give us a good future. Out of Your good will You choose to bless us, and when You bless us, You do not add sorrow to it.

You want us to live abundant lives, lives overflowing with Your blessings. Help us realize that to enjoy Your blessings, we must walk with You, Lord. Give each of us a mind that desires to know You more, a heart that overflows with love for You, and a will that submits to Your sovereign will.

We know, Lord, that if we seek after You, then all other blessings will follow. May we walk into the blessings of the tribes that You have made available to us through Your Son, Jesus Christ. All along the way, help us keep our eyes on You and not on the blessings, Lord.

You are good, You are gracious, You are compassionate and You are merciful. We thank You for who You are, Almighty God.

In Jesus' name we pray, Amen.

1

Reuben

Happy are those who are stable,
for nothing can stop
their blessings from God.

While I was studying in Bible college, I had a few very close
friends. We used to spend time praying together, playing cricket
and sharing meals. We would also share our individual passions
for the Kingdom of God in India. The day came when we gradu-
ated, and we all moved to different places to minister. After
many long years, I was invited to speak in a large gathering in a
certain city in India. There was one particular friend from my
Bible college days who lived in this city. I had lost touch with
him over the years, so the moment I reached the city I was eager
to meet him.

When I inquired about him, I found that he had left the ministry and had become an alcoholic, walking the streets. I was so
shocked that I cried and prayed for him. My posters had been
put up all over the city, and this friend saw them and came for
the meeting. The moment I spotted him, I ran to him, hugged

him and cried. He looked so different—so shabby and unkempt, with a long beard. I asked him why he had become like this. He replied that he had been hurt in the ministry and just could not decide to stay in it. All that passion, all that potential wasted because he could not make up his mind to stand strong. Today, I still pray for him.

The Bible tells us how instability in the life of Jacob's firstborn son, Reuben, robbed him of the blessings that were rightfully his. His father told him that he missed out on the blessings of the firstborn because of his unsteady character. Later on, Moses had no blessing at all to pronounce over the tribe of Reuben and only offered a prayer for them.

Many people today have so much talent and so many dreams of achieving greatness, but they are stagnant—stuck in the same position for years—because of instability in their lives. Like the cold frost that kills the buds, instability can cause grave damage and prevent us from achieving our God-given dreams.

In the book of Revelation Christ tells the Laodicean church, "I know your deeds, that you are neither cold nor hot. I wish you were either one or the other!" (Revelation 3:15). Here are a few more Bible verses about instability:

> The seed that fell among thorns stands for those who hear, but as they go on their way they are choked by life's worries, riches and pleasures, and they do not mature.
>
> Luke 8:14

> Jesus replied, "No one who puts a hand to the plow and looks back is fit for service in the kingdom of God."
>
> Luke 9:62

> Then we will no longer be infants, tossed back and forth by the waves, and blown here and there by every wind of teaching and by the cunning and craftiness of people in their deceitful scheming.
>
> Ephesians 4:14

Elijah went before the people and said, "How long will you waver between two opinions? If the LORD is God, follow him; but if Baal is God, follow him."

1 Kings 18:21

Like a muddied spring or a polluted well are the righteous who give way to the wicked.

Proverbs 25:26

As we look further into what the Bible teaches about instability and understand that God desires for us to have a stable character, we will begin to set right our ways and walk into the blessings that God has planned for us.

The Birth of Reuben

Genesis 29 narrates the story of Jacob being deceived by Laban, his uncle, into marrying Leah instead of Rachel, the girl he loved and had asked to marry. He had already worked for Laban seven long years for Rachel. The time seemed to go by quickly; the wait and the work were not difficult because his love for Rachel was so great. Imagine how disappointed and disheartened Jacob was when he discovered that Laban had given him the eldest daughter, Leah, in marriage instead of Rachel. Not willing to lose Rachel, he worked another seven years for her.

Jacob ended up taking both sisters as his wives. He really loved the one, while the other had been forced upon him. This resulted in various problems for the family. Both wives struggled for their husband's love, and they attempted to make each other jealous. Life must have been depressing and frustrating in that household.

Leah may have been unloved by her new husband, but God did not ignore her. God favored her by opening her womb and blessing her with children. The Bible tells us,

> When the LORD saw that Leah was not loved, he enabled her to conceive, but Rachel remained childless. Leah became pregnant and gave birth to a son. She named him Reuben, for she said, "It is because the LORD has seen my misery. Surely my husband will love me now."
>
> Genesis 29:31–32

The footnote in my Bible is quick to add that the name Reuben means, "See, a son." It is as though Leah, filled with joy, looks at the child in her arms and says with great delight, "Wow, I have a son!"

What stands out here is that Leah is very conscious of God's concern for her, and she gives Him all the credit. She acknowledges that God Himself witnessed her pain and suffering, and that He gave her a son to help her overcome her misery. Leah further expresses confidence that since she bore a son even before Rachel, her husband would at least love her now.

Just for that moment, what joy Leah must have experienced. She was certain her husband finally would pay attention to her. The birth of Reuben brought his mother such great joy.

Reuben as a Young Man

The next time we read about Reuben in Scripture, he is venturing out into the fields as a boy. He may have gone out to play or to help with some small chores. While in the fields, he notices some mandrake plants. He gathers them and brings them to his mother, and Leah uses them to trade for her husband's affections (see Genesis 30:14–16).

One wonders whether, for a boy of his young age, Reuben was already aware of the significance of those plants. We do not know if he realized that they could help a barren woman conceive, or if he just happened to see them and innocently thought it might be nice to give them to his mother.

Either way, the little boy grew up. Things changed as he grew into a passionate young man. Just after the death of Rachel in

Genesis 35, we see that Reuben was unable to control his passions. Jacob (also called Israel by then) settled in Migdal Eder, and while he was living there, "Reuben went in and slept with his father's concubine Bilhah, and Israel heard of it" (Genesis 35:22). Bilhah was Rachel's servant, and by then Rachel had given her to Jacob to bear children for her (see Genesis 30:1–8). Bilhah definitely would have been grieving the death of Rachel, and Reuben must have taken advantage of her in that situation.

When Moses gave the people of Israel the Law later, he warned against sins of the sort that Reuben had committed (see Leviticus 18:6–8). Reuben dishonored his father through his act, and although Jacob heard about it and did nothing immediately, surely he was upset. A moment of uncontrolled desire therefore cost Reuben his privileges as the firstborn son of Jacob.

Reuben and Joseph

You probably are familiar with the story of how much the sons of Jacob disliked their brother Joseph because of his dreams in which they all bowed down to him. They also disliked him because they saw how much their father, Jacob, favored Joseph over the rest of them. The Bible says that they hated him so much that they could not even speak a kind word to him. When the opportunity arose, they plotted to kill him. They threw him into a cistern and lied to their father, saying that a wild animal had killed him (see Genesis 37). In this context, we read about Reuben again. This more mature Reuben seems to have changed. For someone who formerly could not control his passions, Reuben not only thinks straight himself, but he also tries to help his other brothers control their own hateful passions. Look at his reaction when he hears them plotting to kill Joseph:

> When Reuben heard this, he tried to rescue him from their hands. "Let's not take his life," he said. "Don't shed any blood. Throw him into this cistern here in the wilderness, but don't lay a hand

on him." Reuben said this to rescue him from them and take him back to his father.

Genesis 37:21–22

Reuben's words and intentions seem noble in this instance. Notice that he desired to save Joseph. He did not want bloodshed, and he intended to return to the cistern later and restore Joseph to their father.

The once uncontrolled Reuben was displaying signs of positive change. Apparently, he was not with his brothers when they decided to sell Joseph to the Ishmaelite merchants. Returning to the cistern to find it empty, Reuben tore his clothes, which symbolized his grief. Then he confronted his brothers and cried out, "The boy isn't there! Where can I turn now?" (Genesis 37:30).

Note Reuben's desperation in asking, "Where can I turn now?" Obviously, there has been a change in his life, and we know it is sincere because we notice its effects on him again later. Jacob sends his ten sons to Egypt during the famine in Canaan, but he keeps back the youngest, Benjamin, not wanting anything to happen to him. I will talk a little more about this story in chapter 4 when we look at Judah's blessings, but let me summarize it briefly here. In Egypt, Joseph had become a high-ranking ruler in the land, second only to Pharaoh. None of his brothers knew this, of course, having sold him into slavery. When the sons of Jacob appeared before him to buy food during the famine, Joseph recognized his brothers and accused them of being spies. He had Simeon seized and put in prison, while demanding that the others return home and bring back their younger brother, Benjamin, whom they had mentioned to him.

During these events, the brothers realized that all this trouble had come upon them because of the way they had treated Joseph. Reuben spoke up at that point, telling them, "Didn't I tell you not to sin against the boy? But you wouldn't listen! Now we must give an accounting for his blood" (Genesis 42:22).

Returning to their father, Jacob's sons told him all that had happened in Egypt and that they must take Benjamin back with them to prove their innocence and rescue Simeon. Jacob vehemently refused, saying that he already had lost two of his sons, Joseph and Simeon, and would not risk losing Benjamin.

Again Reuben spoke up with strong words, this time addressed to his father rather than his brothers: "You may put both of my sons to death if I do not bring him back to you. Entrust him to my care, and I will bring him back" (verse 37).

Reuben expressed no doubt at all in his words. Confidently he said, "I will bring him back." He was willing to risk the lives of both his own sons on it, which normally no father would do. He was saying to Jacob, "Trust me; I will bring Benjamin back to you. If I don't, you may kill my sons."

That was the level of confidence Reuben displayed. Evidently, something had taken place in Reuben's life that had brought about this change in him. It may have been that his repentance brought the grace of God into his life. Sensing there was a good cause behind this transformation, Moses later speaks life into the tribe of Reuben and pleads for them before God.

Another mention of Reuben takes place in Genesis 46:9, when he is listed in passing, along with his sons, among all those who went with Jacob into Egypt. And finally, there is an interesting mention of Reuben when Joseph goes to see their father, Jacob, who is sick on his deathbed. With all his remaining strength, Jacob shares with Joseph all that God had promised him. He further adds that the two sons born to Joseph in Egypt before Jacob's arrival there would become his:

> Now then, your two sons born to you in Egypt before I came to you here will be reckoned as mine; Ephraim and Manasseh will be mine, just as Reuben and Simeon are mine.
>
> Genesis 48:5

I think this is a fascinating comparison. Jacob seems to be saying that although Reuben may have lost his privileges as the firstborn, he still considers Reuben his son. After what Reuben had done by dishonoring his father, Jacob could have disowned him. Instead, he asserts that Reuben is still his son. This is grace! Reuben did not deserve his father's love, but Jacob still chose to love him.

Jacob's Prophetic Words over Reuben

When Jacob called his sons to gather round so he could speak about what would happen to them in the future, imagine the excitement and curiosity they must have felt as they all came running to their father. He called out to Reuben first, and though he still loved him as a son, the words he had for him were not at all promising. They sounded more like a curse:

> Reuben, you are my firstborn, my might, the first sign of my strength, excelling in honor, excelling in power. Turbulent as the waters, you will no longer excel, for you went up onto your father's bed, onto my couch and defiled it.

> Genesis 49:3–4

Compare the wording in *The Message*, a version of the Bible that I enjoy using and often refer to because it adds clarity and understanding to many scriptural passages:

> Reuben, you're my firstborn, my strength, first proof of my manhood, at the top in honor and at the top in power, but like a bucket of water spilled, you'll be at the top no more, because you climbed into your father's marriage bed, mounting that couch, and you defiled it.

Jacob began by stating all Reuben had meant to him as his firstborn. Reuben symbolized Jacob's might and strength. He should have been assisting his father, helping him carry his responsibilities and standing along with him, by his side—all the privileges of being firstborn. Among all of Jacob's children, Reuben could have held the highest place of honor and power. The rest should have respected Reuben the most.

While all of this was Reuben's birthright, he lost it because he chose to disrespect his father by defiling one of Jacob's concubines, Bilhah (see 1 Chronicles 5:1). He did not stop even for a moment and consider the consequences of his evil act. Jacob may have kept quiet when the incident took place, but on his deathbed he let Reuben and all his other sons know that such a sin could not and would not be ignored. Jacob concluded that Reuben's turbulent and unstable spirit had robbed him of his spirit of excellence. Reuben's instability ended up costing him everything that rightfully belonged to him.

Moses and the Tribe of Reuben

Jacob's prophetic words over Reuben clearly indicated that Reuben's future held nothing of promise. That turned out to be true. During the time of Deborah the judge, Israel faced a great threat from the Canaanites and went to battle against them. Most of Israel joined hands with Deborah, but not the Reubenites. In her song of victory after defeating the Canaanites, Deborah had only this to say about the tribe of Reuben: "In the districts of Reuben there was much searching of heart. Why did you stay among the sheep pens to hear the whistling for the flocks? In the districts of Reuben there was much searching of heart" (Judges 5:15–16).

The Reubenites had potential, but they did not use it. When the call had come to join in the fight, the Reubenites were completely undecided about what they should do. They were unstable indeed! They lost their position of honor and power, and they lost their opportunity to influence their nation's future.

It did not end there on a hopeless note for the tribe, however. Just as Jacob had graciously acknowledged Reuben as his son even after his terrible sin, God Almighty would also acknowledge the positive transformation that had taken place in Reuben's life. Look at Moses' prayer over the tribe of Reuben:

> Let Reuben live and not die, nor his people be few.
>
> Deuteronomy 33:6

The Message says it this way:

> Let Reuben live and not die, but just barely, in diminishing numbers.

Interceding on behalf of the Reubenites, Moses implored God not to wipe them out totally. God in His grace preserved the tribe and let them live, letting them exist even though they played no important role in Israel's history.

Yes, the Reubenites simply existed; they did not excel. In that way, both Reuben and his tribe stand out as a reminder to us that we are not to take God-given privileges for granted. We must keep in mind that in one moment of instability, it is possible to lose out on the destiny that God has planned for us.

Today's Application for Us

Let's look at another reminder in Scripture about the consequences of instability. We read in Judges 13:5 that God had chosen Samson not just as a judge and deliverer, but also as "a Nazarite, dedicated to God from the womb." Samson's parents were overjoyed at the angel's announcement about his birth, and his father, Manoah, was careful to inquire of the Lord about how to raise the boy (see Judges 13). Having received instructions from God, I believe Samson's parents must have taught their son the way a Nazarite should live. But Samson's life shows us that he had the same issue as Reuben—instability. Even though Samson was of the tribe of Dan, not Reuben, he had a lot in common with Reuben and his unstable ways.

God had instructed the Israelites that they were not to intermarry with non-Israelite nations. Although Samson was a Nazarite set apart for God, he went against God's law and expressed a desire to marry a Philistine girl (Judges 14:1–4). The

Lord used this situation to confront the Philistines, who were ruling over Israel, but intermarriage clearly was not His direction for the Israelites. Neither was Samson to touch or eat anything unclean, yet the Bible tells us that he took honey from the carcass of a lion he had killed and ate it (Judges 14:8–9). He also gave some to his parents, but he did not tell them it had come out of a dead animal.

Samson was not stable enough to decide between the things of God and the things of this world. Sometimes the Spirit of the Lord would come upon him and he would suddenly become an instrument in the hands of God. Other times he would not have the stability to refrain from acting according to his own will.

The New Testament gives us another example of the consequences of instability. In his letter to Philemon, we see the apostle Paul talking about Demas as his fellow worker, and he also makes mention of Demas in his letter to the church at Colossae (see Philemon 24; Colossians 4:14). But later on, Paul's words to Timothy show us a different picture that brings to light the unstable mind of Demas: "Do your best to come to me quickly, for Demas, because he loved this world, has deserted me and has gone to Thessalonica" (2 Timothy 4:9–10). Demas was beginning to accomplish so much for the Kingdom of God, and then he lost his ministry because of the instability of his commitment.

The lives of Reuben, Samson and Demas clearly depict for us how our instability can result in our downfall. How do we overcome instability? We will look at some specific ways to do that in a moment, but basically, stability comes through listening to and obeying the voice of our Master. Look at the comparison Jesus makes in Matthew 7:24–27 between stability and instability:

> Therefore everyone who hears these words of mine and puts them into practice is like a wise man who built his house on the rock. The rain came down, the streams rose, and the winds blew and beat against that house; yet it did not fall, because it had its foundation on the rock. But everyone who hears these words of

mine and does not put them into practice is like a foolish man who built his house on sand. The rain came down, the streams rose, and the winds blew and beat against that house, and it fell with a great crash.

Relying on God Brings Stability

There was a time in my ministry when I experienced some confusion and instability over an important decision. My church congregation had grown to four hundred people, and we were in need of a larger place. The members wanted to know when I would buy the land for our new church building. The price of land at that time was exorbitant, and I had no funds or sponsors. I was confused about what to do.

During this time of instability, I went on three days of fasting and prayer. The noise of the people was starting to get to my head. Some of them were hesitant to come to our church or become members because of this issue. I got on my scooter and drove to a secluded place thirty kilometers away to pray. My heart's cry to God was for stability to do the right thing at this crucial time.

That was when God spoke to me, saying He would give me a miracle land. After that, my mind was strong in God and sensitive to the guidance of the Holy Spirit. The next Sunday, I came to church and preached from my heart. I asked the congregation to speak these words in faith: "Where is the land? The land is there. Where? There."

At the end of the service a businessman came and asked, "Pastor, please tell us, where is the land?"

I told him, "I don't know where it is, but what I do know is that God will give us a miracle land."

Within a week's time, an elderly person called me and gave me a gift of land so that we could build our church where it is presently situated. It was my reliance on God that enabled me to do the right thing at that time of instability.

Ways to Overcome Instability

We read in Scripture that Methuselah lived 969 years and then died (see Genesis 5:27). The only remarkable thing about his life is that he lived the longest of anyone before or after him. It is saddening to see how so long a life failed to accomplish anything beyond a few verses of mention in the Bible. Unlike Methuselah, our lives must be progressive. For the glory of God, we must excel in all we do. That requires stability on our part. Here are some things we have learned about instability from the examples we looked at in Scripture:

- Instability can cause us to make the wrong choices.
- Instability can cause us to give priority to the things of the world rather than the things of God.
- Instability can cause us to fall short of fulfilling our calling and potential.

We need to live lives that are stable. Here are some ways through which we can achieve a life of stability:

Destroy the past. As the apostle Paul says in Philippians 3:13–14, "One thing I do: Forgetting what is behind and straining toward what is ahead, I press on toward the goal." We need to burn any bridge that connects us to negative things of the past, and we need to look forward and not allow anything to hold us back from accomplishing the goals God has for us.

Dedicate ourselves to understand the purpose of God in our lives. "Therefore, I urge you, brothers, in view of God's mercy, to offer your bodies as living sacrifices, holy and pleasing to God—this is your spiritual act of worship" (Romans 12:1 NIV1984). We should not let the things of the world distract us. Rather, as Paul urges, we need to surrender our lives to God and let Him lead us.

Determine to be around people who are stable. "Walk with the wise and become wise, for a companion of fools suffers harm" (Proverbs 13:20). The people around us invariably tend to influence our thoughts and actions. We need to be careful about whom we allow to influence us.

Discipline ourselves to achieve projects within a given deadline. Paul says, "I strike a blow to my body and make it my slave so that after I have preached to others, I myself will not be disqualified for the prize" (1 Corinthians 9:27). We need to train ourselves so that we will not be slack or procrastinate about the tasks set before us. We need to live as winners.

Develop spiritual character through a systematic walk with God. We need to challenge ourselves to read the Bible at least one hour a day, because great men of God have disciplined themselves to read the Word of God systematically. We need to regularly attend a church where we will grow spiritually in God. As the writer of Hebrews says, "Let us not give up meeting together, as some are in the habit of doing, but let us encourage one another—and all the more as you see the Day approaching" (Hebrews 10:25 NIV1984). We also need to spend time in prayer and serve others in the way that Christ showed Himself as a servant leader: "Do your best to present yourself to God as one approved, a worker who does not need to be ashamed and who correctly handles the word of truth" (2 Timothy 2:15).

As we see constantly in the Word of God, unstable people have been unproductive and have never been a blessing to His Kingdom. Unstable people look at the prosperity of others and wish that they had such blessings, but they never learn to live a life of stability that would bring such blessings on them. As we have learned from Reuben and the Reubenite tribe, instability will hinder the unlimited blessings of God in our lives. Let's commit ourselves to avoid instability, and let's ask God to give us a spirit of stability in all that we do.

Let's Pray Together

Our gracious and loving heavenly Father, we want to thank You for teaching us from the life of Reuben that we should never lose our God-given opportunities by allowing our selfish desires to take control. We should never allow instability in our lives, because it destroys the blessings You have for us.

Strengthen us through the power of the Holy Spirit, and give us a spirit of stability so that we can live a victorious life for Your glory.

In Jesus' name we pray, Amen.

2

Simeon

Happy are those who control their anger,
for they will not be scattered.

Graham Staines came to India with his family and worked with great burden and passion among the lepers in Orissa. His two young sons, Philip and Timothy, studied at Hebron School in Ooty at the same time that my children studied there. During one vacation, his boys left school to spend some time with their parents and sister. Graham and the boys were traveling in a jeep one night during this vacation and decided to take a break along the way. Planning to sleep in the vehicle, Graham parked it and they settled in for some rest. When the three of them were fast asleep, a mob approached and set the jeep on fire, burning Graham and his sons alive.

One man, the instigator of the mob, had not liked what Graham was doing as a Christian missionary. Acting in a moment of haste, this angry man got a mob all worked up and convinced them to commit this cruel and heartless act. Even when the father and sons tried to escape the burning vehicle, the angry mob would not allow them to climb out. The three of them died a painful death. One man's anger resulted in the loss of three innocent lives!

Holding on to anger is like keeping fire on your lap and trying to live with it. You cannot do it; it will burn up everything you have built. That is what we will learn from the story of Simeon and his tribe. It is a story about how anger and fits of fury can cost a man his joy, his blessings and his destiny. Simeon was a man who struggled with anger, and eventually it cost him all the blessings that God had prepared for him. His father, Jacob, could only pronounce a curse on him, and Moses literally had nothing at all to speak over Simeon's tribe.

Anger has been causing problems for a long time. Even today, it seems to cause most of the problems we face in our world. Anger breeds hurt, bitterness, hatred, jealousy and violent actions—the very things that God detests. Writing to the church in Galatia, the apostle Paul lists "hatred, discord, jealousy, fits of rage, selfish ambition, dissentions, factions" (and several other things) as obvious acts of the flesh or a sinful nature. He goes on to warn that "those who live like this will not inherit the kingdom of God" (Galatians 5:19–21). Look at what else the Bible has to say about anger:

"In your anger do not sin": Do not let the sun go down while you are still angry, and do not give the devil a foothold.

Ephesians 4:26–27

A quick-tempered man does foolish things, and a crafty man is hated.

Proverbs 14:17 NIV1984

Do not be quickly provoked in your spirit, for anger resides in the lap of fools.

Ecclesiastes 7:9

But now you must also rid yourselves of all such things as these: anger, rage, malice, slander, and filthy language from your lips.

Colossians 3:8

My dear brothers, take note of this: Everyone should be quick to listen, slow to speak and slow to become angry, for man's anger does not bring about the righteous life that God desires.

James 1:19–20 NIV1984

If we get a grasp on the warning that Paul so clearly gives the Galatian church, and if we take the teaching in God's Word seriously, we will begin to deal with the devastating emotion of anger in our lives.

The Birth of Simeon

Simeon was the second son of Leah and Jacob, born just after Reuben. The Bible tells us that Jacob loved Leah's sister, Rachel, more than he loved Leah (see Genesis 29:30). This must have been very difficult for Leah, who considered herself unloved and rejected by her husband. It also caused great strife between the two sisters, who eventually had to battle the hurt, bitterness and jealousy that arose between them.

Watching all this brewing in Jacob's family, God decided to intervene. "When the Lord saw that Leah was not loved, he opened her womb, but Rachel was barren" (Genesis 29:31 NIV1984). Leah started giving birth to children, while Rachel looked on with envy.

After giving birth to her firstborn, Reuben, Leah conceived again and gave birth to another son, of whom she said, "Because the LORD heard that I am not loved, he gave me this one too" (Genesis 29:33). For that reason she named her second son Simeon, which simply means "the One who hears."

Leah recognized the favor of God on her life, especially in enabling her to have children while her sister remained barren. When Leah acknowledged that the Lord had heard how she was unloved, it seems to imply that she took her pain and struggle to Him in prayer and was overjoyed when He answered her. It gave her assurance to know that God had heard her cry.

Simeon and the Shechemites

The next time we read about Simeon in the Bible, it is in connection with the cruel massacre of the Shechemites. Jacob and his family had traveled from Paddan Aram to the city of Shechem in Canaan, and Jacob bought some land from the family of Hamor, the ruler of the area, and pitched his tent there (see Genesis 33:18–19). His only daughter, Dinah, who also was born to Leah, decided to venture out into the city. Her beauty drew the attention of Shechem the son of Hamor, who first raped her and then told his father of his desire to marry her (see Genesis 34).

Jacob was alone when he heard that Dinah had been defiled, and at first he chose to keep quiet about it. But his sons, filled with anger, came in from the fields where they were working as soon as they heard what had happened to their sister. Meanwhile, Shechem's father, Hamor, came to talk to Jacob about his son marrying Dinah. Hamor and his son expressed their willingness to compensate for what had happened to the girl. They offered to give Jacob and his sons anything they wanted.

All that Jacob's sons asked of them was that every male in the Shechemite clan be circumcised. Both Hamor and Shechem eagerly accepted this condition, and Shechem immediately went to convince his fellow townsmen at the city gate to comply. The men agreed, and soon all of them were circumcised. Three days later, they were still groaning in pain.

It is in this context that we read about Simeon. Unable to accept their sister Dinah's disgrace, he and his brother Levi decided to take revenge and claim their sister back by killing every male in the city of Shechem, even though most of them were innocent. The rest of the brothers joined in plundering the city. They carried away everything, including the Shechemites' belongings, their riches, their women and their children.

Jacob's response to the entire situation was saddening. He mainly feared the response of the Canaanites and others who were living in that land. His only concern was that he and his household would be destroyed—a selfish response indeed!

The response of Simeon and Levi was no better. They chose to destroy their names for the sake of pride and were defiant in their actions. When Jacob accosted them, their response was simply, "Should he have treated our sister like a prostitute?" (Genesis 34:31). Simeon and Levi acted in a fit of rage, purely seeking revenge. This one incident caused them to lose not only their privileges, but also their father's blessings.

Simeon in Egypt

After the unfortunate incident at Shechem, we next read about Simeon at the time of the great famine in Canaan, when Jacob sent his sons to buy grain in Egypt. This was some time after they had decided to kill their brother Joseph, but with Reuben's intervention had thrown him into a pit instead. Then, on Judah's suggestion, they had sold him to Ishmaelite traders and lied to their father, saying Joseph had been killed by a wild animal (see Genesis 37).

Needing to buy grain from Egypt, Jacob decided to keep young Benjamin back, fearing for his safety, while he sent his other ten sons to Egypt. Because of God's favor, by this time Joseph had risen to become second only to Pharaoh in power. On seeing his brothers, Joseph soon recognized them, while they failed to recognize him. To test them, Joseph repeatedly accused them of being spies and put them in custody for three days, despite their pleas of innocence. He then set them free on the third day, on the condition that one of them stay behind in the prison while the rest returned home to bring back their youngest brother, Benjamin, whom they had spoken about earlier. Choosing a hostage from among them, Joseph "had Simeon taken from them and bound before their eyes" (Genesis 42:24). The rest of the brothers traveled home and later came back with Benjamin. Seeing his youngest brother safe, Joseph was convinced that his brothers had indeed changed, so he released Simeon back to them (Genesis 43:23).

It is unclear from the Bible text whether Joseph chose Simeon randomly as his detainee, or whether he kept Simeon because he feared that this brother might do something hasty in his tendency toward anger. There is the possibility that as Joseph reflected on his experience of being thrown into the pit, nearly being murdered by his brothers and then being sold into slavery, he was aware that Simeon was the most short-tempered brother of them all.

While the brothers were all in Joseph's custody and were still unaware of who he was, they expressed regret among themselves at what they had done to their brother Joseph. They believed that they were in trouble because of it and said to each other, "Surely we are being punished because of our brother. We saw how distressed he was when he pleaded with us for his life, but we would not listen; that's why this distress has come on us" (Genesis 42:21). Eventually, Joseph revealed himself to his brothers and everything was resolved between them. He invited his whole family to come and live in Egypt. The last time Simeon's name is mentioned is in the list that records the families who migrated there with Jacob (see Genesis 46:10).

Jacob's Prophetic Words over Simeon

The most important thing to note about Jacob's prophetic words over his son Simeon is that he has nothing good to tell him about his future. Jacob has no blessings to declare over him. With a heavy heart, Jacob states that his second son, Simeon, who could have taken hold of all the privileges of the firstborn since Reuben had lost them, would only be cursed, along with Levi:

> Simeon and Levi are brothers—their swords are weapons of violence. Let me not enter their council, let me not join their assembly, for they have killed men in their anger and hamstrung oxen as they

pleased. Cursed be their anger, so fierce, and their fury, so cruel! I will scatter them in Jacob and disperse them in Israel.

Genesis 49:5–7

The Message translates the passage like this:

Simeon and Levi are two of a kind, ready to fight at the drop of a hat. I don't want anything to do with their vendettas, want no part in their bitter feuds; they kill men in fits of temper, slash oxen on a whim. A curse on their uncontrolled anger, on their indiscriminate wrath. I'll throw them out with the trash; I'll shred and scatter them like confetti throughout Israel.

Jacob addresses these two sons together. (We will talk more about Levi in the next chapter.) Consumed by their anger, these two had cruelly vented their fury on the Shechemites. Jacob sees them as self-willed men who could not control their anger and who chose to express it violently. *The Message* makes it appear that like Levi, Simeon was someone who was just waiting for a fight. Every little chance, he would pick up a quarrel. That was one thing that came so easily to him that he did not have to work hard at it.

Jacob makes it clear that he does not want to be part of these boys' quarrels, grudges and revenge. He wants nothing to do with them; he does not even want to be in their company, for he knows that it will only bring him more disgrace. It was not even safe to be around them, because if they suddenly got angry, they did not hesitate to kill innocent people and harm animals heartlessly. Such was Simeon's anger, and such anger is indeed sin displeasing to God. It can only be cursed.

In his prophetic words over these two sons, Simeon and Levi, Jacob seems to imply that people with uncontrolled anger should not be together, for the havoc they wreak will be doubled. The best thing is that they be scattered. The prophetic words Jacob had for Simeon were that in the future he would indeed be scattered and would have little or no influence at all in Israel.

Moses and the Tribe of Simeon

We can see the fulfillment of Jacob's prophecy over Simeon as we trace the history of Israel. When the tribes of Israel were numbered at Sinai after the Exodus, the Simeonites numbered 59,300 men (see Numbers 1:23). They were one of the largest tribes at that time. After the plague, at the second census God commanded Moses to take, the tribe of Simeon had decreased in count to 22,200 men (see Numbers 26:14). One of the obvious reasons for such a decrease was the Simeonites' immorality and idolatry, for which Zimri, the leader of a Simeonite family, was held responsible and killed (see Numbers 25:14).

Like Jacob with his son Simeon, Moses did not have any positive prophetic words to speak over the tribe of Simeon—not one word. He did not even mention them at all in his blessings! The only thing that Moses assigned to the Simeonites was to stand on Mount Gerizim with some other tribes and bless the people:

> When you have crossed the Jordan, these tribes shall stand on Mount Gerizim to bless the people: Simeon, Levi, Judah, Issachar, Joseph and Benjamin.
>
> Deuteronomy 27:12

Due to its small numbers, the tribe of Simeon was allotted a place within the tribe of Judah because what was allotted to Judah was more than the Judaites needed. The two tribes helped each other when they needed to attack their enemies, but the tribe of Simeon did not grow as great in number as the people of Judah (see Joshua 19:1–9; Judges 1:3–17; 1 Chronicles 4:27).

The prophecy of Jacob over Simeon was fulfilled. The Simeonites were scattered throughout the towns of Judah and therefore had nothing substantial to contribute to the history of Israel on their own. Simeon is a prime example of the fact that great people with great opportunities can destroy their future because of their anger.

Today's Application for Us

Pastor and evangelist Robert H. Schuller once said, "Doomed are the hotheads! Unhappy are they who lose their cool and are too proud to say, 'I'm sorry.'" This has been true from the start. After the fall of Adam and Eve, Satan used anger as a weapon to bring division between their sons Cain and Abel. Genesis 4 records the very first murder in the Bible, and the cause behind it was Cain's anger.

Cain and Abel were both favored of God, but they had different livelihoods. Cain was a farmer who "worked the soil," and Abel was a shepherd who "kept flocks" (Genesis 4:2). Each brought different offerings to the Lord. The Bible tells us that Cain brought some of the fruits of the soil, while Abel brought fat portions from some of the firstborn of his flocks. All seemed well between the brothers until this moment. We are not told of any competitive spirit, anger, bitterness or grudges between them. Yet when God's favor rested on Abel and his offering and not on Cain and his offering, Cain could not accept it. His pride was hurt, his anger started to rise and he became disheartened.

An amazing thing many fail to notice here is that the Lord saw what was happening inside Cain and knew how he was going to react. In order to keep him from falling into sin, the Lord spoke to him, saying, "Why are you angry? Why is your face downcast? If you do what is right, will you not be accepted? But if you do not do what is right, sin is crouching at your door; it desires to have you, but you must master it" (Genesis 4:6–7).

Even though God had rejected Cain's offering, He did not reject Cain. Out of His great love, He gave Cain an opportunity to make the right choice. God was telling Cain that he must master his thoughts and overcome sin. If Cain had rectified his ways before God and had asked Him for the reason why his offering was not accepted, God would have ministered to him. Then Cain would have been able to enjoy the favor of God, as Abel did. But Cain's anger took control and he decided on his own course of action, which led him to murder Abel.

Never make an important decision when you are angry and your spirit is not aligned with the Holy Spirit. If Cain had taken some time to exercise self-control, perhaps Abel himself would have helped him bring the Lord an acceptable offering.

Our Lord Jesus spoke powerful words condemning anger in His Sermon on the Mount. He goes deeper than the action, to evaluate the attitude. He points out that while the Law of Moses condemns the action of murder and subjects a murderer to judgment, even the one who is guilty of anger will be judged. Anger uncontrolled leads to murder. In the teachings of Jesus, an angry person faces the danger of the fire of hell (see Matthew 5:21–22).

In the early Church, we read that the Holy Spirit asked that Barnabas and Paul be set apart for a special assignment (see Acts 13:2). The Church prayed over the two of them and released them to do the Lord's work. Together these two men traveled through parts of Asia Minor preaching the Gospel. After a fruitful ministry, they returned and reported all that the Lord had done. Later, Paul called Barnabas to revisit with him the churches they had established. Then they had a difference of opinion about whether or not John Mark should go with them, and Scripture tells us, "They had such a sharp disagreement that they parted company" (Acts 15:39). Rather than combining their powerful ministries, they were scattered from each other for a time, which takes us back to Jacob's prophecy over his two angry sons, Simeon and Levi.

I remember the well-known story of Alexander the Great, who killed his close friend Cleitus, a man who earlier had saved Alexander's life in war. This is one example of how anger can come between the best of friends and completely destroy a friendship. What Alexander did in that moment of anger he regretted till his own death.

Focus on the Family founder James Dobson once said, "Satan's most successful maneuver in churches and Christian organizations is to get people angry at one another, to attack and insult our brothers and sisters, thus splitting the body of

Christ." This is obvious in the Church and even in the world. People so easily get angry with one another today. I asked my students in a Bible study class to answer the question, "What is the one thing that gets you angry the most?" Their answers varied widely:

- When they are overstressed or overworked
- When people misuse their name
- When people treat them unfairly
- When people they trust let them down
- When people use them and then dump them
- When they are misunderstood
- When irresponsible people fail to meet their expectations
- When they are blamed and have done nothing wrong
- When they are unable to forgive others who have wronged them
- When people misinterpret the truth
- When people do not demonstrate right values
- When people twist their words
- When people disrespect them and their decisions
- When people speak against them
- When they are forced to do something they do not like
- When people undermine their authority
- When people question their integrity

The list can go on. Notice how even small things can deeply offend people. Things within them make them angry, and things others do to them also make them angry. Anger for whatever reason, especially when uncontrolled, can cause great damage. It can take away your joy, torment you every day and destroy your important relationships. An angry person will only be scattered, as Simeon and Levi were, and will find it difficult to maintain a healthy relationship with anyone.

Focus on God, Not Anger

It is imperative that as believers, we learn how to deal with and overcome anger. There have been many times in my ministry when anger could have taken hold of me, and I dread to think what the result could have been. During my early years in ministry, I had a desire to encourage people. Because of that, I trusted some people too quickly and gave them vital responsibilities in the church. These same people eventually split the church, taking more than 70 percent of the members with them. Of a congregation with 150 members, they took away more than 100 people. This was disturbing! I felt like bulldozing every one of them for what they had done to me. I felt helpless because I was new to the place, did not have any friends and did not have any other money coming in to support myself. I literally went through shame, starvation and intense suffering as a result. I came to the place where I began to question whether God really had called me to pioneer the church.

In this desperate situation, I decided that I would not defend myself and would not challenge or fight with the ones who had split the church. Instead, I started spending a lot of time in the presence of God. I did this for over six months. As I began to reflect on my ministry, my hurt and my relationship with God, I realized that the more I worked among people, the more opportunity I would have to become hurt and angry. God then spoke clearly to me, telling me that although I was working among people, my call to serve came from *Him*. That revelation brought great healing in my spirit. I realized that I was not to serve people; I was to serve God. This helped me take my anger to the Lord instead of expressing it toward other people.

From that time on, I began to focus on building a strong relationship with God and building the church. My change of focus not only helped me avoid living in anger; it also helped me minister with a greater anointing of the Holy Spirit. As a result, at present our church has grown to over 25,000 people in attendance every Sunday. I realized that my priority was my calling to preach the

Word of God in the nation of India, bringing souls to the knowledge of Christ. Harboring anger would only make me lose my peace with God and my impact on the nation.

Your anger can bring about a downfall in your life or ministry. Anger can destroy you and the people around you. It can destroy the call of God on your life. You and I cannot stop people from hurting us and stirring up our anger, but we must learn to refrain from dealing with them out of our angry feelings. Instead, we need to focus on God and commit the situation into His mighty hand, knowing fully well that He is a God of mercy who will help us.

Ways to Overcome Anger

We all must learn to deal with and overcome our anger. Let me suggest several ways in which we can do so. Carefully think through these different ways, knowing that God will help you apply each one to the challenges you face in the area of anger.

Reflect on whether the problem started with you. Have you done something wrong or said something that instigated the problem, which in turn rebounded? Deal with yourself first, before dealing with the person or persons who made you angry.

Refrain from ignoring your anger. Don't try to push your anger under the carpet or ignore it and act as though nothing is wrong. Accept the fact that you are upset or angry, and determine that you will deal with it in the right way. Realize that as a believer, you must learn to manifest the fruit of the Spirit in every trying situation.

Rest in the presence of God. Worship the Lord, because worship will enable you to take your eyes off your problems and focus on His attributes instead. Read the psalms, because in most of them the psalmists take their anger and frustration to God and ask Him for His help. Fast and pray, for only with the help of the Holy Spirit will you be able to conquer the flesh and the sinful tendencies within you (see Romans 8:1–2).

Release the person or persons who wronged you into the hands of God. Forgive them and begin to bless them. You can heal a wound with medicine, but you cannot heal words spoken in anger. Be careful about the words you speak into a situation, for "the tongue has the power of life and death" (Proverbs 18:21).

Realize the hand of God on your life and in your ministry. Don't allow what happened to stagnate your progress or rob you of your relationship with God. Don't let it cause you to lose the anointing on your life. Have no doubt in your mind that God will complete in your life all that He has called you to accomplish. "He who began a good work in you will carry it on to completion until the day of Christ Jesus" (Philippians 1:6).

Let's decide to root out from our hearts the spirit of anger that can lead to sin and destruction. Let's resolve never to allow the devil to destroy the call of God on our lives.

Let's Pray Together

Dear Lord Jesus, we come into Your presence and ask You to touch our lives. Lord, we pray that You will help us overcome our struggle with the sin of anger and unforgiveness.

Lord, help us deal with our anger and be released from its bondage. We pray that You will deliver us and set us free. Help us not to lose the abundant blessings You have for us, as Simeon lost his blessings, just because of the sin of anger.

Be by our side, Lord, and help us live a victorious life!

In Jesus' name we pray, Amen.

3

Levi

Happy are those who stand up for the Lord,
for their curse will be turned into a blessing.

A young girl born into a good Christian family was raised up with godly values and principles. She regularly attended a good church and grew in God's Word. Then she fell in love with a non-Christian boy. Her parents pleaded with her, saying that if she went ahead with her choice she would be going against the Word of God, which clearly says that a believer should not marry an unbeliever. This girl's pastors, her family and her friends all tried to reason with her, but she stubbornly decided to marry the boy. She was adamant about it, in spite of knowing that she would be going against God with her choice.

This young lady willingly chose to compromise her principles and beliefs. She went ahead and married the boy she loved. On the very first day of her married life, her troubles started. She was forced to follow her husband's ideals, and her life changed completely. She suffered a great deal because she had not stood for God, but had compromised her beliefs instead.

Genesis 34 relates the story of Levi, Jacob's third son, who also chose to go his own way rather than God's way. Along with his brother Simeon, Levi mercilessly committed murder and greatly displeased his father through that act. On his deathbed Jacob cursed Levi for his anger, saying that Levi and Simeon would be scattered throughout Israel. That prophetic word was fulfilled, although the curse was reversed for the Levites in Deuteronomy 33, where Moses blesses the tribe of Levi for standing up for God so zealously at Mount Sinai and for prioritizing Him above their own families. As we will see from our look at Levi and his tribe, choosing to stand up for the Lord is vitally important if we are to receive His blessings in our lives.

Toward the end of his earthly journey, Joshua gathered the tribes of Israel at Shechem and challenged them to renounce their idolatry and follow the Lord, who brought them out of Egypt. He asked them to make a definite choice between Yahweh and the gods of the other nations. His own decision, he told them, was to serve the Lord faithfully. Joshua 24:15 records his words: "But as for me and my household, we will serve the LORD." Here are a few more Bible verses about standing strong for God:

I am astonished that you are so quickly deserting the one who called you to live in the grace of Christ and are turning to a different gospel.

Galatians 1:6

Do not be yoked together with unbelievers. For what do righteousness and wickedness have in common? Or what fellowship can light have with darkness?

2 Corinthians 6:14

If anyone, then, knows the good they ought to do and doesn't do it, it is sin for them.

James 4:17

Do not turn to the right or the left; keep your foot from evil.

Proverbs 4:27

Do not love the world or anything in the world. If anyone loves the world, love for the Father is not in them. For everything in the world—the lust of the flesh, the lust of the eyes, and the pride of life—comes not from the Father but from the world. The world and its desires pass away, but whoever does the will of God lives forever.

1 John 2:15–17

At times we may compromise on things in our lives that seem small and insignificant to us. We need to be aware that our decisions at every point of compromise determine whether we will receive or obstruct our blessings from God. Let's talk about Levi and some of the choices he made that obstructed the blessings of God in his life. Then we will talk about some heroes of faith in the Bible who stood strong for God in the face of great peril. From these examples, I think we will discover that God expects us to be true to Him in every area of our lives and to strive to live lives that are faithful to Him. Making good choices pleases and glorifies Him, and it also releases His choicest blessings into our lives.

The Birth of Levi

The jealousy and strife between Jacob's wives, Leah and Rachel, kept building over the years. God had opened Leah's womb, and she had given birth to Reuben and then Simeon. Now she had a third child on the way.

During all the time that Leah was bearing children, Rachel must have kept telling herself not to worry, for surely she would soon have children herself. While Leah was being blessed, Rachel must have been waiting with great expectancy for her blessing.

With the birth of her firstborn, Reuben, Leah had expected her husband to love her, but it did not happen. With the birth of Simeon next, Leah had expressed her disappointment that Jacob still did not choose to love her. But she also expressed joy that God had heard her cry of dejection and had chosen to bless her again.

The Lord's favor continued to rest on Leah: "Again she conceived, and when she gave birth to a son she said, 'Now at last my husband will become attached to me, because I have borne him three sons.' So he was named Levi" (Genesis 29:34).

Another son, another blessing from God, another opportunity to win her husband's affection. Having given birth to three sons, Leah felt that this third time her husband certainly would notice her and pay more attention to her, at last becoming more attached to her. Levi's birth instilled great hope in Leah.

Levi and the Shechemites

Levi was the younger brother of both Reuben and Simeon, but somehow he was drawn to Simeon, who was closest to him in age. We talked in chapter 2 about how together these two brothers had wreaked havoc on the Shechemites for defiling their blood sister, Dinah (see Genesis 34). Let's look more closely at Levi's part in this vicious act. There are two possibilities why he may have gotten involved. First, Simeon may have managed either to convince or to pressure Levi into accompanying him. Levi may have just gone along with his big brother, doing whatever Simeon asked. Second, maybe Levi himself was incensed with anger over what had happened to their only sister. Maybe he was also consumed with a desire for revenge, and the two brothers had chosen to deal with righting the wrong themselves.

Whatever the reason Levi accompanied Simeon, he did something evil and cruel that day. Together, he and Simeon mercilessly killed every male in the city of Shechem. They even put Hamor and Shechem himself to death as they claimed their sister back from Shechem's house (see Genesis 34:25–26). Levi did not try to stop his brother Simeon; the two of them simply took justice into their own hands and went on a murderous rampage.

For this act that Levi committed without a second thought, he was cursed along with his brother. Their father, Jacob, chose to speak to Levi and Simeon as one because of their oneness in bringing destruction on the Shechemites.

Further on in the book of Genesis, Levi is not mentioned by name at all in the story of the sons of Jacob plotting against their brother Joseph. But obviously, he was present with his brothers when they sold Joseph into slavery and when they later visited Egypt during the famine. Neither is Levi's name mentioned in the rest of Genesis after this incident, other than appearing in the list of those who accompanied Jacob to Egypt (see Genesis 46:11). The book of Exodus does tell us how long Levi lived: "These were the names of the sons of Levi according to their records: Gershon, Kohath and Merari. Levi lived 137 years" (Exodus 6:16).

Jacob's Prophetic Words over Levi

The words Jacob speaks over Levi are the same that he speaks over Simeon. They are unhappy words, disappointing words, words that condemn Levi for his anger and ruthless deeds. Let's read them once more:

> Simeon and Levi are brothers—their swords are weapons of violence. Let me not enter their council, let me not join their assembly, for they have killed men in their anger and hamstrung oxen as they pleased. Cursed be their anger, so fierce, and their fury, so cruel! I will scatter them in Jacob and disperse them in Israel.
>
> Genesis 49:5–7

Speaking about the future of Levi's descendants, Jacob says they will be scattered just like the Simeonites. This prophecy was indeed fulfilled. The Levites were not assigned a particular portion when the people of Israel settled in Canaan. They were scattered in 48 cities throughout Israel, not settling all together in one place like the other tribes: "In all you must give the Levites forty-eight towns, together with their pasturelands" (Numbers 35:7). Of these towns, six would be cities of refuge to which a person who had accidentally killed someone could flee (see verse 6).

In keeping with the words of Jacob, the Levites were dispersed throughout Israel. Yet while the Levites were scattered like the Simeonites, there was a difference between them. The Simeonites exerted no influence and slowly disappeared, but not so with the Levites. They are mentioned all through the Old Testament as carrying great responsibility and having immense bearing on the history of Israel. The events that took place around Mount Sinai in Moses' time will show us why.

Moses and the Tribe of Levi

Moses had no words to speak over the tribe of Simeon, yet surprisingly, he had much to say about the Levites. He spoke these words of promise and blessing over them:

> Your Thummim and Urim belong to your faithful servant. You tested him at Massah; you contended with him at the waters of Meribah. He said of his father and mother, "I have no regard for them." He did not recognize his brothers or acknowledge his own children, but he watched over your word and guarded your covenant. He teaches your precepts to Jacob and your law to Israel. He offers incense before you and whole burnt offerings on your altar. Bless all his skills, LORD, and be pleased with the work of his hands. Strike down those who rise against him, his foes till they rise no more.
>
> Deuteronomy 33:8–11

The Message reads like this:

> Let your Thummim and Urim belong to your loyal saint; the one you tested at Massah, whom you fought with at the Waters of Meribah, who said of his father and mother, "I no longer recognize them." He turned his back on his brothers and neglected his children, because he was guarding your sayings and watching over your Covenant. Let him teach your rules to Jacob and your Revelation to Israel, let

him keep the incense rising to your nostrils and the Whole-Burnt-Offerings on your Altar. God bless his commitment, stamp your seal of approval on what he does; disable the loins of those who defy him, make sure we've heard the last from those who hate him.

While referring to the "Thummim and Urim," which were the two stones that the high priest used during certain times to find the will of God, Moses seems to indicate that the Levites were favored of God and given the solemn responsibility of the priesthood. A grave responsibility indeed! What was it that brought God's favor on the Levites? Moses makes it clear that it was their loyalty to God and their willingness to stand up for Him.

The incident Moses is recollecting when he gives the Levites his blessing happened at the foot of Mount Sinai, when Moses had gone up the mountain to commune with God. Having received the Ten Commandments, he came down only to find the people of Israel, led by Aaron himself, immersed in their idolatry. This angered God and He decided to destroy them, but Moses interceded on their behalf. In the scene that awaited Moses when he reached the camp, notice the Levites' reaction:

> Moses saw that the people were running wild and that Aaron had let them get out of control and so become a laughingstock to their enemies. So he stood at the entrance to the camp and said, "Whoever is for the LORD, come to me." And all the Levites rallied to him.
>
> Then he said to them, "This is what the LORD, the God of Israel, says: 'Each man strap a sword to his side. Go back and forth through the camp from one end to the other, each killing his brother and friend and neighbor.'" The Levites did as Moses commanded, and that day about three thousand of the people died. Then Moses said, "You have been set apart to the LORD today, for you were against your own sons and brothers, and he has blessed you this day."
>
> Exodus 32:25–29

It was this act of standing up for what was right that won the Levites the blessings of Moses and the favor of God. The Lord told Moses,

"I have taken the Levites from among the Israelites in place of the first male offspring of every Israelite woman. The Levites are mine" (Numbers 3:12). Because of the Levites' uncompromising loyalty toward God, He chose to make them His and give them the position and privileges of the firstborn that Reuben and Simeon had lost.

We see this same attribute of standing up for God in the Levites again in Numbers 25, when the people of Israel found themselves in a similar situation. In Shittim the people again became engaged in idolatry and immorality, along with the Moabites. God's anger burned against His people, and Moses called all the leaders of Israel and told them that God wanted them to put to death everyone within their camp who was sinning against Him. At that time Phinehas, a Levite, saw the Simeonite leader Zimri bringing a Midianite woman into his tent. Immediately, Phinehas stood up for what was right:

> When Phinehas son of Eleazar, the son of Aaron, the priest, saw this, he left the assembly, took a spear in his hand and followed the Israelite into the tent. He drove the spear into both of them, right through the Israelite man and into the woman's stomach.
>
> Numbers 25:7–8

This pleased the Lord, and He turned His anger away from the Israelites, saying to Moses,

> Phinehas son of Eleazar, the son of Aaron, the priest, has turned my anger away from the Israelites. Since he was as zealous for my honor among them as I am, I did not put an end to them in my zeal. Therefore tell him I am making my covenant of peace with him. He and his descendants will have a covenant of a lasting priesthood, because he was zealous for the honor of his God and made atonement for the Israelites.
>
> Numbers 25:11–13

Once again it was a Levite who did not hesitate to stand up for God. It is interesting to note in this incident that Phinehas was a descendant of Levi, and Zimri was a descendant of Simeon—the two brothers who were cursed by their father, Jacob. At Shechem the two brothers were united in their sin, but here a Simeonite continued sinning, while a Levite opposed sin. What a change in the Levites! No wonder that in his blessing of the Levites, Moses called on God to bless all the work of their hands and ensure that no enemies would rise up against them.

In accordance with the prophecy of Jacob over his sons Simeon and Levi, the Levites were indeed scattered. Yet the main difference between the Levites and the Simeonites later on was that the Levites repented and chose to stand for God, with no compromise. Moses saw the loyalty they displayed time and again, and hence blessed them. A curse turned into a blessing, and a tribe that could have disappeared with no impact on their fellow men rose in position and honor with God instead. The Lord Himself declared that they would be His and that He would be their inheritance (see Numbers 18:20).

Today's Application for Us

Taking a stand is never easy, especially because the temptation to compromise is often strong. As difficult as it can be to take a stand, however, we have learned from the Levites that it brings with it the blessings of God. In another example from the Bible, we read the story of three friends, Shadrach, Meshach and Abednego. They were among the captives from Judah whom King Nebuchadnezzar had brought to Babylon. King Nebuchadnezzar made a golden image of himself and issued this decree: "Whoever does not fall down and worship will immediately be thrown into a blazing furnace" (Daniel 3:6).

The king's decree was clear and firm. Everyone had to bow down to this image or risk being thrown into a blazing furnace. The three friends would not bow down, however, so they were taken before the king. He gave them one more chance to choose: Either they could compromise and obey man, which would mean disobeying God and His Law, or they could obey God and disobey the king, who was threatening to throw them into a blazing furnace. Their answer to the king was as clear and firm as his decree:

> If we are thrown into the blazing furnace, the God we serve is able to deliver us from it, and he will deliver us from Your Majesty's hand. But even if he does not, we want you to know, Your Majesty, that we will not serve your gods or worship the image of gold you have set up.
>
> Daniel 3:17–18

One word that stands out strongly in their response is the word *serve*. These young men were totally unwilling to serve anyone other than the Great I Am, in whom they trusted. In other words, they would not compromise; they would stand up for God to the point of death. But God proved to them that as His Word says, He is an unfailing God who answers the cry of the one who is in trouble (see Psalm 34:6).

Likewise, we must be unfailing in serving God by our refusal to compromise over what is right. Jesus said, "No one can serve two masters. Either you will hate the one and love the other, or you will be devoted to the one and despise the other. You cannot serve both God and money" (Matthew 6:24). His words imply that if we attempt to serve both God and man, or God and money, invariably we will end up compromising.

We see another scriptural example of standing up for God in the New Testament story of Peter and John. After the infilling of the Holy Spirit, the disciples began to proclaim the Gospel, which was accompanied by signs and wonders. As people saw the sick being healed and delivered, many began to believe in Jesus, and the Church began to grow. The priests, the captain of the temple guard and the Sadducees were alarmed at this, so they not only arrested Peter and John, but also "commanded them not to speak or teach at all in the name of Jesus" (Acts 4:18).

That left Peter and John with a choice to make. They could either compromise or take a stand for the One they believed in. Their answer was also clear and firm: "Which is right in God's eyes: to listen to you, or to him? You be the judges! As for us, we cannot help speaking about what we have seen and heard" (Acts 4:19–20). Their choice was to preach and teach about Jesus despite the warnings, threats and even their arrest on several occasions.

Choosing to Stand for God

I recall one of our mass evangelism crusades in India among the people of Punjab. We saw God move in a supernatural way. Many of the Punjabis were being saved, healed and delivered. At that time, a militant nationalist group started opposing the crusade and started to spread panic among the people, raising up slogans against us and beating up those who tried to stop them. They wanted to find their way to the stage in order to harm me and my team.

These militants faked sickness and injury, and thereby pushed their way through the crowds. One group brought a cripple on stage and challenged me to make him walk in Jesus' name. The situation at this point became very tense. The onlookers were wondering what I would do and if the God I had preached about was really able to heal. I could either exercise my faith and pray that the man be healed, or I could compromise and accept defeat. I prayed in faith, and God healed that man. He got up and walked!

On seeing this miracle, the crowd was in an uproar. The militants became angry because of the crowd's reaction, and now they wanted to harm me all the more. My assistant pastors asked me to exit the stage from behind and move to a place where I would be safe. They strongly urged me to get off the stage and save myself. As they were telling me this, I could see the militant group literally pushing their way forward. I had to make a choice, and I had to make it fast. I could either heed the voices urging me to run away, or I could take a brave stand for God and remain onstage.

At that moment God strengthened me to make the right choice and stand for Him, even at the risk of losing my life. As a result, we were able to see the power of God move in a greater way in the midst of that severe opposition. We witnessed hundreds of Punjabis giving their life to Jesus that day. It reminded me of my saying, which I firmly believe in and often repeat: "India will be washed by the blood of Jesus!"

Ways We Can Stand for God

We should never compromise. Most often, three things happen when we compromise on what is right:

- We end up making the wrong choice and losing our blessings.
- We do not see the result or outcome we desired.
- We display the absence of courage.

Rather than compromise, we must boldly take a stand for God regardless of probable outcome, because even between the neck and the knife God can do a miracle. Here are some ways through which you can build yourself up so that you will not compromise:

Change your ways in alignment with God's ways, and thereby impact your situation. Peter denied Jesus three times, but still changed his ways and was greatly used by God. Jacob deceived his brother, Esau, but still changed his ways during the course of his journey toward God. He even became someone who prophesied. His name was Jacob, which means a deceiver, but because he changed his ways, God changed his name to Israel, which means a prince with God (see Genesis 32:27–29).

Choose to follow your godly convictions. The prophet Elijah tells this same thing to the people of Israel while at Mount Carmel: "Elijah went before the people and said, 'How long will you waver between two opinions? If the LORD is God, follow him; but if Baal is God, follow him'" (1 Kings 18:21).

Challenge the kingdom of the devil by applying Scriptures from the Word of God. Jesus did the same when the devil tried to tempt Him. The devil tried to tempt Jesus thrice, but each time, Jesus quoted Scriptures saying "it is written" and overcame all Satan's attempts to tempt Him (Matthew 4:1–11).

Continue to live in submission to the Holy Spirit. Although King David disobeyed God and compromised by sinning with Bathsheba, he chose to cry out in repentance, saying, "Do not cast me from your presence or take your Holy Spirit from me" (Psalm 51:11). Seeking another chance with God, David committed himself to live in submission to the Holy Spirit.

Carefully distinguish between the voice of the enemy and the voice of God so that you will not compromise. In the Garden of Eden, Eve had the choice of listening to the voice of God and obeying Him. God had instructed Adam and Eve that while everything in the Garden was at their disposal, the only restriction was that they must not eat the fruit from the tree of the knowledge of good and evil. Instead of listening to God, Eve heeded the deceptive words of the serpent and disobeyed God: "When the woman saw that the fruit of the tree was good for food and pleasing to the eye, and also desirable for gaining wisdom, she took some and ate it" (Genesis 3:6).

People who compromise will struggle to attain their potential, but people who take a stand for God without compromising will receive great rewards and will be blessed. Many people who walk with God, read the Word, pray in tongues and go to church regularly still compromise with the world because they are not sensitive to the voice of the Holy Spirit. They tend to assume that what they are doing is God's will, not realizing that they are failing in God's Kingdom. Being successful in the world does not necessarily mean that we are living in right relationship with God. Kingdom principles require that we live an uncompromising life. May we endeavor to live for Christ and stand for Him without compromise. That is where the blessings are.

Let's Pray Together

Our gracious and loving heavenly Father, we come to You in the name of Jesus. Thank You, Lord, for helping us understand the principles we have learned from the Levites about taking a stand for You and not compromising with the world.

As we are living in this world, where so many people compromise Your principles, help us live a victorious life for You.

We pray that through the power of the Holy Spirit, You will help us overcome the temptation to compromise. Help us make choices every day that bring You glory in every situation.

In Jesus' name we pray, Amen.

4

Judah

Happy are those who repent
of their sins and praise God,
for they shall be exalted above the rest.

It was 1984, and we had around 150 members in our church. With
an unquenchable passion for souls, I was working hard to see an
increase in the numbers. I visited houses incessantly from morning
till night, trying hard to push our church growth up, but I could
see no results.

Then one day God spoke to me, saying, *Do you want to build
the church, or do you want Me to build the church?*

I was shocked. I realized that I had been trying to bring in people
by my own efforts, without depending on God. With a repentant
heart, I decided to spend more time in prayer and reading the Word.
I also decided to leave everything in God's hands.

That Sunday, I made an announcement to the congregation that
I would not be visiting them at home anymore. Many people were
offended and some wanted to leave the church, but I stood firm in
my decision. I bought a table and chair for about Indian rupees
165 (barely $11 USD then), screened off a portion of the church

hall to make a small office and appointed a secretary. Having no other work to give her, I asked her to type the book of Genesis. Disheartened, she quit the job. I informed the people that I was available for appointments, but no one came to meet with me.

I started spending many hours in the presence of God, seeking His face. It was a humble beginning, but God honored my decision to put Him first. He started moving powerfully in the Sunday services, and the people were touched by the Word of God that I preached. The church began to grow, and within six months our attendance had grown to four hundred. As I repented and placed my trust in God, He started doing wonders in our midst.

The book of Jonah in the Bible relates the story of the prophet Jonah, who disobeyed God but later repented and turned back to Him. Disregarding God's command to go preach to the people of Nineveh, Jonah defiantly boarded a ship to Tarshish instead, only to encounter a fierce storm on the way. Knowing that his disobedience was the cause of the storm, Jonah asked the sailors to throw him overboard. When they did so, the raging storm calmed down immediately, and a big fish (prepared by God) swallowed Jonah.

Jonah's repentant heart is apparent as he says, "When my life was ebbing away, I remembered you, LORD, and my prayer rose to you, to your holy temple" (2:7). In the midst of his anguish he looked up to God and praised Him, saying, "But I, with shouts of grateful praise, will sacrifice to you" (verse 9). That instant, the Lord answered Jonah's prayer, and he was free again as the fish deposited him on dry land. He was forgiven and accepted by the grace of God.

The grace of God can pull you out of the deepest sea of sin. The life of Judah, the fourth son of Jacob, is a symbol of God's grace. Judah sinned against his daughter-in-law, Tamar, and then he repented and humbled himself to the extent of saying, "She is more righteous than I" (Genesis 38:26). Consequently, on his deathbed Jacob blessed Judah with kingship, might and prosperity. And in Deuteronomy 33 Moses prayed for the Lord to bless the tribe of Judah.

When Judah repented, God forgave him and blessed him. If we yield our hearts and lives to the Lord, we also will enjoy the unending showers of His blessings. Here are a few verses that speak of God's boundless grace toward those who repent and turn to Him:

Repent, then, and turn to God, so that your sins may be wiped out, that times of refreshing may come from the Lord.

Acts 3:19

If we confess our sins, he is faithful and just and will forgive us our sins and purify us from all unrighteousness.

1 John 1:9

If my people, who are called by my name, will humble themselves and pray and seek my face and turn from their wicked ways, then I will hear from heaven, and I will forgive their sin and will heal their land.

2 Chronicles 7:14

Because your heart was responsive and you humbled yourself before the LORD when you heard what I have spoken against this place and its people—that they would become a curse and be laid waste—and because you tore your robes and wept in my presence, I also have heard you, declares the LORD.

2 Kings 22:19

"Even now," declares the LORD, "return to me with all your heart, with fasting and weeping and mourning." Rend your heart and not your garments. Return to the LORD your God, for he is gracious and compassionate, slow to anger and abounding in love, and he relents from sending calamity.

Joel 2:12–13

Judah and his tribe have much to show us about what God's grace can do in our lives when we turn to the Lord in humble repentance. Let's look more closely at Judah's story, along with his blessings and what they mean for us today.

The Birth of Judah

Enjoying the favor of God, Leah had been blessed with three sons: Reuben, Simeon and Levi. With the birth of each child, all she expected was to win her husband's love and attention. Though despised by Jacob, at least she had borne him sons, while Rachel (the wife whom he so loved) still had no children. After the birth of each son, excitement and hope would rise up within Leah—surely now her husband would love her! Then her hope would slowly fade away, leaving her as disappointed and frustrated as before.

But the Lord did not forget Leah. Once again He blessed her with a son: "She conceived again, and when she gave birth to a son she said, 'This time I will praise the LORD.' So she named him Judah" (Genesis 29:35).

One more son—what joy! On the birth of her fourth son, Leah praises the Lord. Having lost any hope by now of a change in Jacob's heart toward her, she does not express any more yearnings for his affection. Instead, this time she takes her eyes off her husband and focuses on the Lord, the only One who stood with her all along.

In Leah's misery, it was the Lord who saw her. When she was unloved, again it was the Lord who heard her every sob. In her disappointment, it was the Lord who drew near to her. It was the Lord and He alone who was with her through it all. So this time when she bears Jacob another son, Leah chooses to praise God. When things do not happen the way she wants, when she runs out of her own plans, and when all her crying is of no avail, Leah just stops and begins to praise God. In that way, the birth of Judah drew Leah closer to God.

Judah and Joseph

As a young man, Judah began to display leadership qualities early. As we saw in chapter 1, when Jacob's sons decided to kill Joseph because he was their father's favorite, Reuben intervened and helped change their minds by suggesting that they throw the boy into a pit instead. They did so, and then, as they began to eat their meal, they saw some Ishmaelite traders coming their way. That is when we read that Judah spoke up:

> Judah said to his brothers, "What will we gain if we kill our brother and cover up his blood? Come, let's sell him to the Ishmaelites and not lay our hands on him; after all, he is our brother, our own flesh and blood." His brothers agreed.

Genesis 37:26–27

Notice that there is a great difference between Reuben's suggestion and Judah's idea. Reuben seemed more diplomatic; he did not want to anger his brothers, and at the same time he did not speak his heart truthfully. Apparently, he suggested throwing Joseph into the pit so that he could return and rescue him later, but he kept that last part of his plan to himself. On the other hand, Judah was straightforward as he stood up for Joseph. He made his brothers think over what they would achieve by murdering Joseph, who was, after all, their own flesh and blood. Judah appealed to their reason and was able to convince them to go along with his idea and win their support for sparing Joseph's life. A true leader in the making!

We looked already at the story of how the brothers traveled to Egypt for Jacob during the famine to buy grain. They returned to their father with the command from Joseph that they must bring back their youngest brother, Benjamin. We saw in chapter 2 that Simeon remained in prison in Egypt while Jacob's other sons tried to convince their father to send Benjamin back with them, but to no avail. When they had exhausted all the grain they had purchased on the first trip, however, the need arose for them to return to Egypt a second time or starve, because the famine was still so severe. Jacob ordered them to go, and once again it is Judah who speaks on behalf of his brothers:

> Judah said to him, "The man warned us solemnly, 'You will not see my face again unless your brother is with you.' If you will send our

brother along with us, we will go down and buy food for you. But
if you will not send him, we will not go down, because the man
said to us, 'You will not see my face again unless your brother is
with you.'"

Genesis 43:3–5

Judah's words showed that he was firm in his resolve. He simply refused to go back to Egypt without Benjamin because "the man" (referring to Joseph, whom they had not yet recognized) had warned them not to do so.

Jacob regretted the fact that they had even mentioned Benjamin to "the man," and he asks his sons why they had brought such trouble on him by doing it. While the other brothers begin to defend themselves before their father, Judah does not. He speaks again, offering his father a solution:

> Send the boy along with me and we will go at once, so that we and
> you and our children may live and not die. I myself will guarantee
> his safety; you can hold me personally responsible for him. If I do
> not bring him back to you and set him here before you, I will bear
> the blame before you all my life. As it is, if we had not delayed, we
> could have gone and returned twice.

Genesis 43:8–10

Here we see Judah expressing his leadership qualities again. He speaks logically and is able to convince his father to send Benjamin with them, something that Reuben had been unable to achieve earlier. Judah was willing to put himself at risk and take total responsibility.

In the interesting narrative found in Genesis 44, Judah also emerges as the hero. With his convincing words, he is able to move Joseph to reveal his true identity. Joseph has accosted his brothers and accused them of stealing a silver cup from his house. Testing them, he threatens to keep the thief as his slave. Of course, the cup is found in Benjamin's sack, right where Joseph's steward had planted it. At this turn of events, Judah approaches Joseph, reminds him of all that has happened and implores him to have mercy on Jacob. True to his commitment to his father, Judah even offers himself as a slave in Benjamin's place:

> So now, if the boy is not with us when I go back to your servant my father, and if my father, whose life is closely bound up with the boy's life, sees that the boy isn't there, he will die. Your servants will bring the gray head of our father down to the grave in sorrow. Your servant guaranteed the boy's safety to my father. I said, "If I do not bring him back to you, I will bear the blame before you, my father, all my life!"
>
> Now then, please let your servant remain here as my lord's slave in place of the boy, and let the boy return with his brothers. How can I go back to my father if the boy is not with me? No! Do not let me see the misery that would come on my father.
>
> Genesis 44:30–34

It was this response that broke the heart of Joseph. He wept at Judah's persuasive words and then disclosed his identity to his brothers.

Judah had everything in him that speaks of good leadership traits. He did not simply follow the crowd; he chose to stand up for what he thought was right. He was able to appeal to other people's reason and logic. He spoke convincingly. He kept his word even at the cost of his own life. The leadership he displayed earned him his father's trust, so much so that when Jacob decided to travel to Egypt with his family, the Bible tells us that Judah was the one he chose to send on ahead to get directions to Goshen from Joseph (see Genesis 46:28).

Judah and Tamar

Between these narratives we just looked at, in which we see Judah developing leadership skills, there is another narrative in Genesis 38 where we see Judah in a different light. Several things stand out in this chapter of the Bible, which gives us insight into Judah's personal life. Just after selling Joseph to the Ishmaelites, Judah left his brothers and made friends with Hirah, an Adullamite, whom he decided to stay with. Living with a non-Israelite, Judah left behind some of his own people's ways and chose to marry a Canaanite woman. Together they had three sons: Er, Onan and Shelah. But it was not enough to marry a Canaanite woman himself; he further arranged for a Canaanite woman named Tamar to marry his son Er. The Lord saw Er's wickedness, however, and put him to death.

One wonders if Judah failed to bring up his sons in the fear of the Lord. His second son, Onan, was unwilling to listen when Judah reminded him of his responsibility to ensure that his brother Er's name did not die out. Onan did not want any part in it and did not fulfill his responsibility with Tamar to conceive an heir to carry on Er's family line. This earned Onan the judgment of God, like his brother, and he died as well (see Genesis 38:8–10). Since Judah's youngest son, Shelah, was too young to get married, Judah then sent Tamar away to her father's house to wait till Shelah grew up. But Judah was afraid that the same thing that had happened to his two older sons would happen to Shelah if the young man married Tamar (see verse 11).

Later, when Tamar noticed that she had not been given as wife to Shelah even though he had grown up, she came up with a plan to deceive her father-in-law into giving her offspring. Tamar fooled Judah into thinking she was a prostitute at the city gate, and she wisely took his seal, cord and staff from him as a pledge of payment for sleeping with her. Then she disappeared. Three months later, Judah heard that Tamar was pregnant and guilty of prostitution. Filled with anger, he called for her to be burned to death. Tamar produced his belongings as they were bringing her out to be punished and declared that she was pregnant by the man who owned these things. On recognizing his belongings, Judah realized that he was the one at fault for not giving Tamar to his son Shelah. He humbly confessed, "She is more righteous than I" (Genesis 38:26).

In a situation where Judah could have defended himself, condemned Tamar and covered his own fault with convincing words, we see him owning up to his fault and being accountable for all that had happened. We also notice his repentant voice as he took responsibility for what he had done.

Jacob's Prophetic Words over Judah

As a child forgets the reason for his or her tears, the grace of God forgets our past. It is only by His grace that God chose to exalt Judah, a man who was willing to humble himself and repent of his sins. God honored him in the blessings Jacob spoke over him and in the prayer Moses later spoke over his tribe.

After speaking strong, harsh words over three of his sons, Reuben, Simeon and Levi, Jacob pronounces a rich blessing over Judah and declares that greater days await him. He has many things to say to Judah:

> Judah, your brothers will praise you; your hand will be on the neck of your enemies; your father's sons will bow down to you. You are a lion's cub, Judah; you return from the prey, my son. Like a lion he crouches and lies down, like a lioness—who dares to rouse him? The scepter will not depart from Judah, nor the ruler's staff from between his feet, until he to whom it belongs shall come and the obedience of the nations shall be his. He will tether his donkey to a vine, his colt to the choicest branch; he will wash his garments in wine, his robes in the blood of grapes. His eyes will be darker than wine, his teeth whiter than milk.
>
> Genesis 49:8–12

The Message puts it this way:

> You, Judah, your brothers will praise you: your fingers on your enemies' throat, while your brothers honor you. You're a lion's cub, Judah, home fresh from the kill, my son. Look at him, couched like a lion, king of beasts; who dares mess with him? The scepter shall not leave Judah; he'll keep a firm grip on the command staff until

the ultimate ruler comes and the nations obey him. He'll tie up his donkey to the grapevine, his purebred prize to a sturdy branch. He will wash his shirt in wine and his cloak in the blood of grapes, his eyes will be darker than wine, his teeth whiter than milk.

Jacob's prophetic words over Judah show us how much God's grace can change our disgrace. Jacob highlights three things that will take place in Judah's life:

- Judah would be honored and respected by the rest of his brothers. He would be strong and courageous and would fight his enemies, while his brothers bow down before him. Jacob compares Judah first to a lion's cub that comes back victorious after its first kill, and then to a full-grown lion, with the king of beasts signifying his courage and strength. No one would challenge him nor spur him to anger.
- The firstborn right to the throne would be his. While Levi would get the priesthood and intercede for the people, Judah would get the kingship and rule over the people. First Chronicles 28:4 says clearly that God chose Judah as the ruler. The kings would come from Judah, and eventually in the plan of God, the King of kings, the Messiah, would also come from him—the One who would command the obedience of all the nations. Matthew mentions Judah as an ancestor of Jesus in his record of the Messiah's genealogy (see Matthew 1:2–3). Further, Revelation 5:5 describes the triumph of "the Lion of the tribe of Judah," Jesus.
- Judah would enjoy great riches and prosperity. In highly descriptive words, Jacob said that Judah would enjoy great wealth and would be satisfied beyond all measure.

Moses and the Tribe of Judah

The words of Jacob were fulfilled in every detail. All the eminent kings came from the tribe of Judah, and as prophesied, the Messiah descended from this line as well. Truly the repentance of Judah resulted in great blessings on his entire tribe, with all the prophecies about them being fulfilled. All of this was because of the grace of God, which is like a vitamin in the life of the worst sinner.

When it was time for Moses to speak over the tribes of Israel, he chose to pray over the tribe of Judah. His prayer for the tribe was this:

> Hear, LORD, the cry of Judah; bring him to his people. With his own hands he defends his cause. Oh, be his help against his foes!
>
> Deuteronomy 33:7

Or as *The Message* puts it,

> Listen, GOD, to the Voice of Judah, bring him to his people; strengthen his grip, be his helper against his foes.

Moses prayed that God would be attentive to the cry of Judah. He prayed that God's protection would be on the tribe every time they went out, and that God would bring them back home to their people safely. Moses petitioned God that since the tribe of Judah took responsibility for their actions, He would give them more strength. Moses further requested that God would go with them into every battle and help them against all their enemies.

Today's Application for Us

The Word of God repeatedly reminds us that we need to repent of our sinful ways if we are fully to inherit the blessings of God. True repentance brings about great blessings, as we saw in the life of Judah. God gives us ample opportunities to repent, turn away from our sinful ways and lead a life that is pleasing to Him.

We see an example of repentance and blessing in the life of King David, who was of the tribe of Judah. God testified concerning him, "I have found David son of Jesse, a man after my own heart;

he will do everything I want him to do" (Acts 13:22). David was ever obedient to God and acknowledged Him in all his ways, but there was an instance in which he acted in the flesh and ended up disobeying God. As a result, David needed to demonstrate the same sort of humble repentance for sin and willingness to take responsibility as his forefather Judah.

King David had one day seen Bathsheba, Uriah's wife, bathing and had lusted after her. He slept with her, and she conceived. To cover his sinful actions, he had her husband killed, ordering his men to place Uriah on the frontline where the battle was the fiercest and then draw back from him (see 2 Samuel 11).

Of course, God was displeased with King David's actions. He sent the prophet Nathan to confront David. Through Nathan, the Lord reminded David of all He had done for him. He had anointed him king over Israel and Judah. He had delivered him from the hands of King Saul, who was seeking desperately to kill him. He had given him his master's house and belongings. And He added that He even would have given David twice as much, if he had only asked. Then God questioned David with these words: "Why did you despise the word of the LORD by doing what is evil in his eyes? You struck down Uriah the Hittite with the sword and took his wife to be your own. You killed him with the sword of the Ammonites" (2 Samuel 12:9).

On hearing God's words, King David realized his sin and repented. His prayer was, "Create in me a pure heart, O God, and renew a steadfast spirit within me. Do not cast me from your presence or take your Holy Spirit from me" (Psalm 51:10–11).

In the four gospels, we find that Jesus always spoke on repentance. While He had compassion on people, delivered them and healed them, His teaching ministry constantly focused on repentance. As Matthew 4:17 tells us, "From that time on Jesus began to preach, 'Repent, for the kingdom of heaven has come near.'"

Peter was one among the disciples who was very close to Jesus. He was with Him for three and a half years, witnessed all His miracles and heard all His teachings. But by nature, Peter was a coward. Jesus told Peter that he would deny Him three times: "Truly I tell you . . . this very night, before the rooster crows, you will disown me three times" (Matthew 26:34).

Peter was adamant that he would never deny Jesus, but then he went out and did that very thing—three times. What is most important for us to see here is what Peter did afterward: "Then Peter remembered the word Jesus had spoken, 'Before the rooster crows, you will disown me three times.' And he went outside and wept bitterly" (Matthew 26:75). This verse reveals Peter's heartfelt emotion. He realized that he had committed a grave sin and had disowned the One he loved. It also reveals Peter's repentant heart. He realized his mistake and repented. From then onward he was a new man, and once he was empowered by the Holy Spirit, he went on to take a bold stand for Christ and proclaim the Gospel far and wide (see Acts 2).

Repentance Brings Blessings

As I mentioned already, during the early days of my ministry I had the misconception that visiting people would be sufficient to build the church. And that is what I did day after day, but nothing happened. In the end, I was burnt out. I was frustrated. At that time my church service was held in a rented building, for which we had to pay Indian rupees 2,500 every month (which back then was equivalent to $167 USD). The offering we received in that time period hardly amounted to 1,500 rupees.

There was a woman attending our church, however, whom I would visit at home every month (as I did with many people). After our initial greeting she would serve snacks, and I would share the Word and then prepare to leave. She would excuse herself at that time and go into the next room, and soon I would hear the creaking sound of a steel cupboard opening. She would emerge after a few minutes and give me an offering of Indian rupees 1,000. Upon receiving it, I would pray and leave.

The offering from this woman was crucial for me because the church hardly had any money to pay the rent for our building.

These were the times when I often had no salary for several months in a row and was literally living by faith. I visited this lady on the third of every month for three months. The fourth month, I made my routine visit to her house, and after sharing the Word I got ready to leave. Eagerly, I was hoping she would get up and go into the other room so I could hear the sound of the steel cupboard creaking open and could receive her offering when she came back out. But nothing happened. The lady just stood there. I told her twice that I was heading back, and still she did not budge. Then she told me that she had heard some negative things about me and hence did not want to contribute money any longer.

I was hurt. I was angry. I was frustrated. I came straight back to the church and went to the basement to talk to God. *I hate You*, I told Him. *Here I am, starving and struggling to do the ministry, and in the meantime someone has gone and spoken badly about me.*

After I vented out all my disappointment, frustration and anger, God's response to me was simple, yet effective: *Did I call you to do the ministry, or did she call you? While I am doing a miracle for you, why are you going there every month and depending on her for that money? I shut one door so that I can open another. And here you are, knocking on the very door that I've closed!*

God's words were very clear. I knew where I had gone wrong. I repented and prayed for forgiveness. I now knew that my dependency had to be on God and not on people. When God does a miracle through someone, instead of looking at that person, we need to look at God. He is the ultimate Source who meets all our needs.

From that week onward, two new families started coming to the church. Their tithe combined was Indian rupees 1,500 a month, which was 500 more than what I used to receive from that woman. God taught me an important lesson the day I repented. My repentance led to Him opening another new door and blessing me in an unexpected manner. When we trust God, He surely will perform a miracle.

After twenty long years, the same woman whom I once had visited came to my church and stood in line for 45 minutes to get in. She approached me with tears in her eyes and told of her regret over listening to the gossip of others about me. She deeply regretted losing the privilege of being part of such a large and thriving ministry. God had blessed us and had grown the church without her offering, but it was also a blessing to see her again and hear her words of repentance.

Ways to Live a Life of Repentance

Through all of this, I learned three valuable lessons that are applicable both in ministry and in life:

- We need to *realize* when we have done something wrong.
- We need to *repent* and depend on God.
- We need to ask God to *renew* our spirit.

Here are some ways in which we can live a life of repentance and thereby inherit the blessings God has in store for us:

Search *our hearts.* We need to find out where we have gone wrong. Unless we know the area in which we have erred, chances are that we will be unable to rectify the situation and will only continue to make the same mistakes again and again. We need to do as David told his son Solomon:

> Acknowledge the God of your father, and serve him with wholehearted devotion and with a willing mind, for the LORD searches every heart and understands every motive behind the thoughts. If you seek him, he will be found by you; but if you forsake him, he will reject you forever.
>
> 1 Chronicles 28:9 NIV1984

Sacrifice *our lives to do the will of God.* His will must be our priority. We need to deny ourselves and surrender our lives into the hands of God: "Therefore, I urge you, brothers, in view of God's mercy, to offer your bodies as living sacrifices, holy and pleasing to God—this is your spiritual act of worship" (Romans 12:1 NIV 1984).

***Submit** to the Lordship of Christ.* One question we need to ask ourselves is whether we are ruling ourselves or whether Christ is ruling us. We must not resist the Lordship of Christ, but must realize that God knows what is best and only does that which is good for us. "Submit yourselves, then, to God. Resist the devil, and he will flee from you" (James 4:7).

***Seek** more after God and His will for us.* God has a plan for each and every one of us (see Jeremiah 29:11). Our heart's cry must be for more of God—to know what He desires of us and to live in accordance with His will. We will be able to know His will only when we seek after Him. As the writer of Hebrews prays, may God "equip you with everything good for doing his will, and may he work in us what is pleasing to him, through Jesus Christ, to whom be glory for ever and ever" (Hebrews 13:21).

***Seize** the opportunities that God brings our way.* We live in the last days, where we see things like hatred, enmity, rumors of war and the depletion of the earth's natural resources. All these things point to that fact that the Rapture could take place at any moment. We should therefore repent and make good of every opportunity that God gives us. Through our doing that, God will lift us up. Ephesians 5:15–16 urges us, "Be very careful, then, how you live— not as unwise but as wise, making the most of every opportunity, because the days are evil."

God's plans for us are to prosper us. Let's be careful to live in the center of His will at all times, receiving His grace with humble repentance. It is only God's grace that brings about true forgiveness in our lives and saves us. My definition of grace would be this:

G—God's

R—Redeeming

A—Act of

C—Compassion, which is

E—Everlasting

Let's Pray Together

Our gracious and loving heavenly Father, thank You for teaching us from Judah's life and David's life that we need to have a heart of repentance. Reveal to us the specific areas in which we need to repent.

Give us the strength, Lord, to turn away from any sin in our lives. Help us be sensitive to Your will and to the leading of the Holy Spirit.

May we live our lives in submission to You, for the glory of Your name.

In Jesus' name we pray, Amen.

5

Zebulun

Happy are those who accept
the plan of God for their lives,
for God Himself will dwell in their midst.

Once when I had traveled to the Middle East for ministry, I was invited to a large company to share the Word of God with its board of directors and pray for them. The minute I entered the room, God spoke clearly to me: *Tell them not to make the big investment they are planning on doing.*

I did not know anything of the company's plans, but whatever God told me, I told them; then I prayed for them and left. Later, I found out what had happened as a result. God had spoken to them through me about that huge project they were working on, into which they had intended to invest a large amount of money. They were perplexed about how to go ahead after hearing this word from God. Of the twelve board members, seven wanted to heed the God-given warning, while the remaining five wanted to go ahead with their original investment plan.

After much deliberation, one board member spoke up: "The man of God, in spite of having no idea of our plans, has warned us not to proceed. Surely this is from God, and we should listen to it."

Finally, the board arrived at a unanimous decision not to make the investment. Imagine their astonishment when, ten days later, news reached them that the deal was a sham! Because the board had chosen to listen to God, the company was saved from incurring a huge loss. Blessings come to those who accept God's plan.

The gospel of Luke tells us of a young woman who was blessed and highly favored because she accepted God's plan. The angel Gabriel visited Mary to bring her the good news that God had chosen her to give birth to the Messiah, His Son. Mary, a virgin betrothed to be married, submitted herself to God so that He could carry out His plan through her. Though it meant that she would be in danger of being stoned to death for being with child even before she wedded Joseph, Mary was willing to risk it all and take the path heaven had laid out for her. "I am the Lord's servant," she answered Gabriel. "May it be to me as you have said" (Luke 1:38 NIV1984). What joy was hers as she surrendered herself as an instrument in the hands of God, in the fulfilment of His divine plan for mankind.

Jacob's son Zebulun also accepted as God's plan the words that his father spoke over his life. In Genesis 49 we see that Jacob has just a few words to say over this particular son; he only prophesies concerning Zebulun's borders and where his habitation would be. (Notice that Jacob did not bless his sons strictly according to their birth order, so we will follow along with him in the order of his blessings.) On hearing his father's prophecy, Zebulun accepts it as the plan of God. As a result, he and his descendants were blessed with joy and prosperity. Let's look at what some other Bible verses have to say about the importance of God's plan for our lives:

> "For I know the plans I have for you," declares the LORD, "plans to prosper you and not to harm you, plans to give you hope and a future."
>
> Jeremiah 29:11

You need to persevere so that when you have done the will of God, you will receive what he has promised.

Hebrews 10:36

Commit to the LORD whatever you do, and he will establish your plans.

Proverbs 16:3

The LORD Almighty has sworn, "Surely, as I have planned, so it will be, and as I have purposed, so it will happen."

Isaiah 14:24

Many are the plans in a person's heart, but it is the LORD's purpose that prevails.

Proverbs 19:21

As we read in God's Word about the blessings Zebulun and several others received because of their humble compliance with the plan of God, may we determine that we will prioritize His plan for our lives above all our other plans. May we determine in our hearts that we will follow the Light that shines down from heaven.

The Birth of Zebulun

The Bible tells us that after the birth of her fourth son, Judah, Leah stopped having children (see Genesis 29:35). In the meantime, her sister, Rachel, was more and more troubled that Leah had already given birth to four sons, while she herself had borne not even one. Rachel began to trouble her husband, Jacob, in turn, telling him, "Give me children, or I'll die!" (Genesis 30:1). She also gave Jacob her maidservant, Bilhah, to sleep with. Bilhah in turn gave birth to two sons.

Not to be outdone, Leah realized that she had stopped having children and gave her maidservant, Zilpah, to Jacob. Zilpah also bore two sons. These events seem to indicate that both Leah and

Rachel had reached new heights of jealousy and bitterness between them. They were overcome by the desire to outdo each other in bearing children, either themselves or through their maidservants (see Genesis 30:1–24). The situation became quite complex, but perhaps this chart of the sons of Jacob will make it simpler:

Birth Order of Jacob's Sons

Leah (Jacob's first cousin)	Zilpah (Leah's maidservant)	Rachel (Leah's sister)	Bilhah (Rachel's maidservant)
1) Reuben	7) Gad	11) Joseph	5) Dan
2) Simeon	8) Asher	12) Benjamin	6) Naphtali
3) Levi			
4) Judah			
9) Issachar			
10) Zebulun			

(Note that the birth of Jacob's only daughter, Dinah, is not included in this chart. She was born to Leah after Zubulun, but before Rachel bore either Joseph or Benjamin.)

After a period of time God's favor once again came upon Leah, and He reopened her womb. She gave birth to Issachar, her fifth son, whom we will talk about in the next chapter (again, following the order of Jacob's blessings). After Issachar's birth we read, "Leah conceived again and bore Jacob a sixth son. Then Leah said, 'God has presented me with a precious gift. This time my husband will treat me with honor, because I have borne him six sons.' So she named him Zebulun" (Genesis 30:19–20).

Leah saw the hand of God in the birth of Zebulun and acknowledged him as a "precious gift." She supposed that since she alone had borne Jacob six sons, he would at least take notice of her and treat her with the honor that was due her. The birth of Zebulun made Leah expect that Jacob would start treating her right.

Besides the record of his birth, Zebulun is hardly mentioned in Genesis. While he apparently was present, any time mention is made of the "sons of Jacob," it seems that nothing he said or did was significant enough to mention of itself. He was one of Jacob's sons who seemed to fade slowly into oblivion in Scripture. The only other time Genesis mentions Zebulun is in the list of those who accompanied Jacob to Egypt (see Genesis 46:14).

Jacob's Prophetic Words over Zebulun

Jacob had just finished speaking words of promise over his fourth son, Judah, words that pronounced a glorious future ahead for him. The gloom that had been in the air after Jacob had denounced his first three sons, Reuben, Simeon and Levi, had now been replaced by cheer. According to their birth order, the next son in line for Jacob's blessing should have been Dan, but Jacob chose to skip over Dan and four other sons—the three others born to the maidservants, as well as Leah's Issachar—to speak next over his tenth son, Zebulun.

Remember that although Issachar and Zebulun were the fifth and sixth sons of Leah, they were the ninth and tenth sons of Jacob because of the maidservants' four sons, Dan, Naphtali, Gad and Asher. If all this seems confusing, perhaps another chart that lists the order of Jacob's blessings would help. You can compare it to the birth order chart above.

Jacob's Order of Blessing His Sons

Leah's Sons	Zilpah's Sons	Rachel's Sons	Bilhah's Sons
1) Reuben	8) Gad	11) Joseph	7) Dan
2) Simeon	9) Asher	12) Benjamin	10) Naphtali
3) Levi			
4) Judah			
5) Zebulun			
6) Issachar			

It is still unclear why Jacob reversed the order of Issachar and Zebulun, both sons of Leah, in his blessings, or why he blessed these two before four of their older brothers. He may have done this so that he could first finish speaking over the sons of Leah before addressing any of the others. It is also interesting to note that Moses addressed these two sons together, as we will see shortly. Whatever the reason behind Jacob's deviation from the birth order in his blessings, he next calls out to his tenth son, Zebulun, and says this about him:

> Zebulun will live by the seashore and become a haven for ships; his border will extend toward Sidon.
>
> Genesis 49:13

Or according to *The Message*,

> Zebulun settles down on the seashore; he's a safe harbor for ships, right alongside Sidon.

Imagine the excitement that must have been Zebulun's when he heard his father call his name long before his rightful turn. Then imagine his disappointment when he realized that his father had nothing much to say over him, nor were Jacob's words very promising. Zebulun could have chosen to react by complaining, "Is that all for me? That's not fair!" But apparently, he did not. We are not told what he said in response, but it appears that in humility he recognized his father's words as God's very words, declaring that a good future awaited him.

It is amazing that to a seemingly insignificant person like Zebulun, Jacob declares exactly where he will settle down according to the plan of God. This fact points out to us that God does not overlook anyone, even those who may seem insignificant. He has every detail of their lives carved out. Zebulun may have had to live by the sea, but where he settled would become a haven, a safe place and a refuge for those who would come in and go out on the waters. His influence would stretch as far as Sidon, one of the chief cities of the Canaanites (see Genesis 10:19).

The Zebulunites and the Judges

Let's look for a moment at Zebulun's descendants. At a period in the Israelites' history when they were oppressed by the Canaanites under the leadership of Sisera, they called upon God to help them. In response, Deborah, Israel's leader at that time, sent for the commander Barak and said to him,

> The LORD, the God of Israel, commands you: "Go, take with you ten thousand men of Naphtali and Zebulun and lead them up to Mount Tabor. I will lead Sisera, the commander of Jabin's army, with his chariots and his troops to the Kishon River and give him into your hands."

> Judges 4:6–7

Barak gathered the men of these two tribes as God had commanded, and they set out to fight the Canaanite army. With God's help they won the victory, and Deborah and Barak broke out into a song of praise recounting all that had happened (see Judges 5). Deborah took time to express her appreciation for the tribes that cooperated in Israel's efforts to fight the Canaanites. In regard to Zebulun, she said that the men who came from Zebulun were capable leaders who held "a commander's staff" in their hands (Judges 5:14). She also described the Zebulunites as a courageous people who put themselves in vulnerable positions at the frontline of the battle and "risked their very lives" (verse 18).

The people of Zebulun were willing to fight for Israel without flinching. They were a bold, unselfish people who did not hesitate to join hands with the other tribes when the need arose. God in His grace even raised a judge, Elon, from among the Zebulunites to rule for a period of ten years. Sadly, Scripture does not mention much of Elon, other than that he led Israel, died and was buried (see Judges 12:11–12). Nonetheless, the tribe of Zebulun itself stands out as an example of those who can at times rise to the occasion and have great impact on their world.

Moses and the Tribe of Zebulun

As I mentioned, Moses combined the words he spoke over the tribes of Issachar and Zebulun. He had good things to declare over them:

> Rejoice, Zebulun, in your going out, and you, Issachar, in your tents. They will summon peoples to the mountain and there offer the sacrifices of the righteous; they will feast on the abundance of the seas, on the treasures hidden in the sand.
>
> Deuteronomy 33:18–19

The Message says it this way:

> Celebrate, Zebulun, as you go out, and Issachar, as you stay home. They'll invite people to the Mountain and offer sacrifices of right worship, for they will have hauled riches in from the sea and gleaned treasures from the beaches.

Moses calls out to the Zebulunites to be joyful, for they will have every reason to celebrate—the main reason being their prosperity, both spiritual and material. Not only will they offer right sacrifices to God that are pleasing to Him, but they also will bring people to the Mountain, meaning to the presence of God. Their location and their trade will enable them to influence many others. They also will enjoy great riches, for all the wealth and treasures of the seas and sand will belong to them.

Far greater than these blessings, however, would be a blessing the inhabitants of that area by the sea would take delight in many years later, as prophesied by Isaiah:

> Nevertheless, there will be no more gloom for those who were in distress. In the past he humbled the land of Zebulun and the land of Naphtali, but in the future he will honor Galilee of the nations, by the Way of the Sea, beyond the Jordan—
> The people walking in darkness have seen a great light; on those living in the land of deep darkness a light has dawned.
>
> Isaiah 9:1–2

The future of Zebulun's tribe was bright indeed. Abundant blessings awaited them in their future, and God Himself would be in their midst. In fulfillment of Isaiah's words, we read in Matthew 4:12–14 that on hearing about the imprisonment of John the Baptist, Jesus decided to go to Galilee:

> When Jesus heard that John had been put in prison, he withdrew to Galilee. Leaving Nazareth, he went and lived in Capernaum, which was by the lake in the area of Zebulun and Naphtali—to fulfill what was said through the prophet Isaiah.

It was there that Jesus started preaching repentance: "From that time on Jesus began to preach, 'Repent, for the kingdom of heaven has come near'" (Matthew 4:17). He invested much of His time ministering to the people in that area. Because Zebulun had accepted the place God had given him in His sovereign plan, his future descendants enjoyed having God Himself in their very midst.

Today's Application for Us

Accepting God's plan, as Zebulun did, brings His presence and promises into our lives. In the Bible, we can learn from others who also had great impact on their world because they accepted God's plan. Consider the story of Noah. During his time, humanity had become terribly wicked. God was greatly displeased to see that "every inclination of the thoughts of the human heart was only evil all the time." In fact, He "regretted that he had made human beings on the earth, and his heart was deeply troubled" (Genesis 6:5–6).

God decided He would destroy not just the human race, but also the animals, birds and other creatures that moved on land. Except for one thing: "Noah found favor in the eyes of the LORD" (Genesis 6:8). God can use the smallest people to do the biggest things. He told Noah about His plan to destroy humankind, and He instructed him to build an ark and gave him the plans to construct it.

Now Noah faced a dilemma—whether to accept the plan God was presenting to him and go ahead with building the ark, or whether to be conscious of the people around him and what they would say, considering the fact that there was no rain and yet he would be building an "ark." Logically, building a giant boat could not have seemed like a wise thing to do.

Noah accepted God's plan even before there was any rain to validate it in the eyes of those watching him. "Noah did everything just as God commanded him" (Genesis 6:22). Here, Noah serves as the epitome of obedience. Though he could not see with his earthly eyes the practicality of God's divine plan working out well, he was able to see with his spiritual eyes that God's plan was foolproof and that He was more than able to make it happen. As Job expressed to the Lord, "I know that you can do all things; no purpose of yours can be thwarted" (Job 42:2).

God gave Noah a divine architectural plan, which Noah then had to execute with the skill of a learned, qualified architectural engineer. Noah was to construct the ark according to the design God had given him. God even intended to place a male and a female of every living creature inside the ark, so the plan included provision for them. To accomplish such a task, God chose an ordinary man who was righteous and blameless and who walked faithfully with Him (see Genesis 6:9). The beauty of the plan was that Noah did not have to work alone. God was with him all along the way.

Jesus told His disciples, "Whoever wants to be my disciple must deny themselves and take up their cross and follow me" (Mark 8:34). Here, the phrase "deny themselves" implies that a person must let go of whatever plans he or she has and instead accept God's plans. After stating this, Jesus added a question: "What good is it for someone to gain the whole world, yet forfeit their soul?" (verse 36).

We can see total acceptance of God's plan clearly demonstrated in the life of the apostle Paul. Initially, Paul (then known as Saul) was a devout Jew and a persecutor of the early Church. Saul's plan was to travel around to find the disciples of Jesus and then persecute them:

> Meanwhile, Saul was still breathing out murderous threats against the Lord's disciples. He went to the high priest and asked him for letters to the synagogues in Damascus, so that if he found any there who belonged to the Way, whether men or women, he might take them as prisoners to Jerusalem.
>
> Acts 9:1–2

Saul was on his way to Damascus when he had an encounter with the Lord. He did not know who was talking to him when he first heard Jesus' voice, so he asked, "Who are you, Lord?" (Acts 9:5).

"I am Jesus, whom you are persecuting," was the reply. "Now get up and go into the city, and you will be told what you must do" (verse 6).

Saul was obedient in doing what he was instructed. In the meantime, the Lord also spoke to a disciple named Ananias, who expressed his fear about meeting Saul. He had heard numerous reports about Saul's persecution of the Church (see verses 13–14). God then revealed to Ananias the plan He had for Saul, and how that which He intended to do through Saul's life was far greater than what Ananias could perceive. He said to Ananias, "Go! This man is my chosen instrument to proclaim my name to the Gentiles and their kings and to the people of Israel" (verse 15).

Ananias obeyed God and went to pray for Saul in person. Saul, now a changed man, firmly believed in the Lord Jesus Christ and accepted the plan of God for his life. He went on to become the apostle Paul, an ardent pioneer and church planter who traveled far and wide fearlessly proclaiming the Gospel of Christ. In fact, Paul became the apostle who wrote most of the New Testament epistles.

Clearly, God was with Noah and Paul, who accepted His plan for their lives. From their example we see the impact we can have when we give our lives to Him.

At the Crossroads

During my second year in Bible college, I started having a burden to spend more time in God's presence in prayer and in reading the Word. At that time, there was a casuarina grove (a garden of ever-green trees and shrubs) just opposite the college. A small bush in that place became my prayer altar. I used to go there every day and spend time in prayer. It was during my time of prayer in that grove that God revealed to me that He wanted me to pioneer a church in Bangalore. The area He showed me consisted of the most affluent people in the society. When I told my father that God wanted me to pioneer a church in Bangalore, he did not want me to stay there. He wanted me to come back to Madurai, where he was located, and help him in the ministry.

This brought me to a crossroads where I had to decide whether I wanted to take the path my heavenly Father had shown me, or take the path my earthly father had shown me. I decided to accept God's plan, but first I prayed that God would once again confirm His plan by having my earthly father give his consent to me pioneering a church in Bangalore. Within a week's time, my father replied to me again, this time expressing his consent to that plan.

I discussed my burden to start a church at Indira Nagar in Bangalore with our local Assembly of God chairman. While he supported me in my ministry, he also warned me about the challenges involved in starting a church in an affluent area. Many who knew of the plan saw me only as a young man with little or no experience who was aiming for the skies and was trying to do the impossible.

God can bless us in the most forsaken place when we stay within His plan. I was a youngster who had just crossed beyond my teen-age years. I had a big vision and a big burden, I was away from the comfort of my family and friends, and I was looking to start a new church among the most affluent people of that society. Yet the only money I had in my hands amounted to 3 rupees (or about 20 cents at the time).

I knew that God had a plan, and I accepted it. While the physical realities around me seemed to make it improbable, the spiritual reality of the impossible becoming possible with God kept me going strong. Today, 34 years later, the same ministry that grew out of that plan has become a church of over 25,000 people, with 85 full-time staff members and 12 services every Sunday in 5 different languages. The ministry is blessing people throughout India and in 40 different countries through live webcasts. Our Sunday services reach 52,000 homes locally through a live telecast on several channels, and we also have established several satellite churches. As Zebulun and the Zebulunites showed us, God is in our midst when we follow His plans.

Ways to Live Out God's Plans

We don't need to be somebody great or amazing to receive the blessings of God. God can use a nobody and make a somebody out of him or her. That process shows us three things about His plans:

- God's plans are *incredible*.
- God's plans are *infallible*.
- God's plans are *irreversible*.

You and I need to live our lives according to God's plans for us. Here are five things you need to do to live a blessed life in the plan of God:

Perceive the God-given plan. You need to understand and be aware of what God is doing in your life. "Do not conform to the pattern of this world, but be transformed by the renewing of your mind. Then you will be able to test and approve what God's will is—his good, pleasing and perfect will" (Romans 12:2). You and I can align our will with God's will and do that which is needed only when we are able to perceive His plan for us.

Purpose in your heart not to allow the devil to destroy God's plan for your life. You need to determine in your heart that no matter what the circumstance might be, you will never allow the devil to get a foothold in your life. "Resist the devil, and he will flee from you" (James 4:7). The devil constantly tries to thwart God's plans and cause our lives to become failures. Never allow that to happen. Always heed the apostle Peter's warning: "Be alert and of sober mind. Your enemy the devil prowls around like a roaring lion looking for someone to devour" (1 Peter 5:8).

Persevere in God's plan even though the going seems tough. God definitely has something in store just for you and just for me. You must persevere regardless of the challenges that might come your way. "Blessed is the one who perseveres under trial because, having stood the test, that person will receive the crown of life that the Lord has promised to those who love him" (James 1:12). It is during times of trial that our true nature is revealed. Never give up, because our God of hope is never too far away.

Prevail in the presence of God. God led the people of Israel with the cloud of glory and the pillar of fire in the wilderness. In fact, Moses told God, "If your Presence does not go with us, do not send us up from here" (Exodus 33:15). They would not go forth without God's presence. In our lives also, God's presence will be with us. He will be the fourth Man in the fiery furnace with us, in the same way that He protected Shadrach, Meshach and Abednego (see Daniel 3:25). The presence of God will overshadow you and me and cover us. It can penetrate the powers of darkness and open up heavenly blessings that we may never have perceived. We will see the miraculous hand of God when we prevail in His presence. And when that happens, it accomplishes the impossible.

Proclaim the promises of God over your life. The promises of God will be the foundation to fulfill the plan of God. You need to hold on to God's promises. Many will speak negative words to you, and you will find many distractions along the way. But His promises will keep you focused. Don't listen to all the voices around you; cling to God's promises instead. His promises will ensure victory. "For no matter how many promises God has made, they are 'Yes' in Christ. And so through him the 'Amen' is spoken by us to the glory of God" (2 Corinthians 1:20).

We need to learn to accept God's plan for our lives, as Zebulun did. God's presence will surround us when we learn to accept His will. When we stay well within the plan of God, He will give us great treasures. The plan of God is greater than the plan of the devil against our lives. God will do that which He has purposed to do through our lives when we accept His plan.

Let's Pray Together

Gracious and loving heavenly Father, we thank You for the good plans that You have for us. Help us surrender our plans to You so that we will understand Your master plan for our lives.

Lord, we choose to trust You and You alone, for we know that You will never fail us. Like Zebulun, we accept Your plans above our own.

We pray that even as we accept and do Your will, Your presence will go with us and You will be in our midst at all times. We promise to live our lives for the glory of Your name.

In Jesus' name we pray, Amen.

6

Issachar

Happy are those who work diligently,
for God will be their reward.

Many years ago, a father I knew brought his son to our home to
stay with us. This young man was not doing well in life, so we took
him in. He used to help us with the household work, and I would
take him with me when I went out to do ministry. I would take him
along to prayer meetings at church or when I went to visit people
at their houses. After the young man had a few years of exposure
to the ministry, I decided to send him to Bible college. I wondered
how he would manage, since he did not have any proper education.
But hoping that he would try his best, I sent him.

   In spite of his limitations, the young man worked very hard in
Bible college. Surprisingly, he got the highest marks in most of his
subjects. He joined a certificate course at first, but went on to do
the diploma course that the college offered. He made the most of
the God-given opportunity he had, worked hard and passed the
course with flying colors. At present, he is one of the pastors on
my pastoral staff. He heads an area of our ministry and is very

much a part of our important meetings and programs. He is happily married and has two children. Although this young man was a person limited by his circumstances, he was in no way idle. He took advantage of the opportunity God brought his way and worked hard, and now God has richly rewarded him.

In his second epistle to the Thessalonians, the apostle Paul expresses his disapproval of idleness in strong terms, saying,

> For even when we were with you, we gave you this rule: "The one who is unwilling to work shall not eat."
> We hear that some among you are idle and disruptive. They are not busy; they are busybodies. Such people we command and urge in the Lord Jesus Christ to settle down and earn the food they eat.
>
> 2 Thessalonians 3:10–12

As we read through the previous chapter to this passage, 2 Thessalonians 2, it becomes clear that false teachers had confused the people by saying that the Day of the Lord was very close at hand. Hearing this, many in the church became idle, refusing to work and disrupting the lives of everyone around them. The apostle Paul reminds the Thessalonians of the time when, along with Silas and Timothy, he had ministered among them. The three of them had worked hard night and day so as not to be a burden to anyone, and Paul urges the church to follow the example they set (see 1 Thessalonians 1:6; 2 Thessalonians 3:6–15).

The Word of God clearly reproves idleness. In prophesying over his son Issachar in Genesis 49, Jacob points out this tendency in him. We will see that he compares Issachar to a strong, well-laden donkey idling between his saddlebags; this son possesses great potential but is too indolent to make use of it. Idleness apparently did not stay part of the tribe of Issachar's heritage, however, which is good. In Deuteronomy 33, Moses will bless this tribe, along with the tribe of Zebulun. Here are a few Bible verses that will encourage us to abandon our idle ways and work hard:

The LORD God took the man and put him in the Garden of Eden to work it and take care of it.

Genesis 2:15

Diligent hands will rule, but laziness ends in forced labor.

Proverbs 12:24

How long will you lie there, you sluggard? When will you get up from your sleep? A little sleep, a little slumber, a little folding of the hands to rest—and poverty will come on you like a thief and scarcity like an armed man.

Proverbs 6:9–11

You will eat the fruit of your labor; blessings and prosperity will be yours.

Psalm 128:2

Whatever you do, work at it with all your heart, as working for the Lord, not for human masters, since you know that you will receive an inheritance from the Lord as a reward. It is the Lord Christ you are serving.

Colossians 3:23–24

Idleness is the barrier that stops the potential in us from flowing out; it can make us ignorant of the greatness that is meant to be ours in Christ. We do not want to idle away our opportunities, as Issachar did. Rather, as we look at the lives of men in the Bible who worked hard, filled with the power of the Holy Spirit—men who did the impossible—let it inspire us to work hard, too, and scale greater heights in every area of our lives.

The Birth of Issachar

Leah kept striving for Jacob's love and attention, while Rachel kept contending to bear him children. Both of them kept struggling for what they so desperately wanted, just to show the other sister that they were able to achieve it. When they failed, they did not give up; they just looked for easier alternatives. When Rachel realized that she seemed unable to bear children, she did not hesitate to give her maidservant to her husband. When Leah realized that she had stopped bearing children, she did not want to be left behind her sister. She, too, gave her maidservant to Jacob. So much struggle, so much confusion and so much pain!

There is an interesting narrative behind Issachar's birth that gives us a glimpse into the kind of tension that existed between these sisters, Leah and Rachel. In chapter 1 we talked a little about how Leah's firstborn, young Reuben, found some mandrake plants in the fields one day and brought them home to give his mother. Rachel saw the mandrakes and pleaded with Leah to give her some. Leah's response to her sister's request revealed all her pent-up anger and frustration: "Wasn't it enough that you took away my husband? Will you take my son's mandrakes too?" (Genesis 30:15). Leah seized this opportunity to let Rachel know exactly how she felt. She literally accused Rachel of snatching her husband away from her, and then she questioned her as to whether she would snatch away the boy's mandrakes, too.

In desperation, Rachel worked out a deal and offered Jacob to Leah for one night in exchange for the mandrakes. The deal sounded good to Leah, and she must have eagerly grabbed it. Imagine the excitement with which Leah must have awaited Jacob's return that evening. On seeing him, she ran up to him and claimed him for the night, saying, "I have hired you with my son's mandrakes" (verse 16).

God saw Leah's desperation in this situation. Hearing her cry, He chose to open her womb: "God listened to Leah, and she became pregnant and bore Jacob a fifth son. Then Leah said, 'God has rewarded me for giving my servant to my husband.' So she named him Issachar" (verses 17–18). To Leah, Issachar was a repayment from God.

We can assume that like Zebulun, Issachar was present whenever Genesis mentions the "sons of Jacob." Just like his brother

Zebulun, however, Issachar is not mentioned specifically by name again in the rest of Genesis, except in the list of those who traveled with Jacob to Egypt (see Genesis 46:13).

Jacob's Prophetic Words over Issachar

Having spoken a few words over Zebulun that had not amounted to much, Jacob now turns his attention to Issachar, the fifth son of Leah, born just before Zebulun. Of this son Jacob says,

> Issachar is a rawboned donkey lying down between two saddlebags. When he sees how good is his resting place and how pleasant is his land, he will bend his shoulder to the burden and submit to forced labor.

Genesis 49:14–15 NIV1984

The Message puts it this way:

> Issachar is one tough donkey crouching between the corrals; when he saw how good the place was, how pleasant the country, he gave up his freedom and went to work as a slave.

For reasons the Bible does not specifically state, Jacob looked at Issachar and called him a donkey—a strong donkey, but one that loved to cease working and rather rest. Jacob may have observed in the past that Issachar liked to take a rest when all his brothers were working.

On hearing these words from his father, Issachar's jaw must have dropped in shameful surprise. He may have thought, *A donkey . . . my father compares me to a donkey, when a little while back he called Judah a lion. . . . Something just isn't right!*

Jacob says that because this son finds a comfortable place for himself and settles in, he will be ruled rather than rule. His words over Issachar seem harsh, but they are for his own good.

It seems that Issachar was foolishly willing to trade his freedom to enjoy a little bit of relaxation. If only he had used the insight and wisdom God had given him more diligently, he could have been a powerful instrument in God's hand, with a greater impact. He also would not have compromised his freedom, being ruled instead of ruling.

The Fighting Men of Issachar

Let's take a look at the descendants of Issachar. Many among them did not share their forefather's idle ways. The Bible mentions that during the time of Deborah, the princes of Issachar went out with her and Barak when they fought the Canaanites (see Judges 5:15). These men of Issachar were not ordinary men; they were noblemen and high-ranking princes. They were the ones who supported Deborah and Barak in the fight; they were described as those rushing into the valley with Barak. Just picture it: Barak leading thousands of men against the Canaanites, with these princes of Issachar rushing into battle for Israel. The men of Issachar did not shrink from their responsibility, nor did they look to see who was behind them or who was by their side. They were loyal, daring and eager to do their part in battle.

A little later God gave a man from Issachar, Tola, the opportunity to rule over Israel as judge for 23 long years. Sadly, like the Zebulunite judge, Elon, nothing of huge significance is noted of Tola's reign (see Judges 10:1–2). What a fine opportunity gone to waste.

The book of Chronicles records that among the men of Issachar were 87,000 fighting men (see 1 Chronicles 7:5). Later, we read that when David was banished from King Saul's sight, many men from the different tribes joined hands with him at Ziklag, until he had a great army. In the list that gives the number of men from each tribe who united with David, the men of Issachar are mentioned this way: "From Issachar, men who understood the times and knew what Israel should do—200 chiefs, with all their relatives under their command" (1 Chronicles 12:32).

While the list records the large numbers in which men from the different tribes came in support of David, there were only 200 men listed from Issachar. Notice, however, two things that were said about these men: First, they were 200 chiefs who brought with them all their relatives under their command, so the actual number of fighting men from Issachar surely would have been many more. Second, these chiefs were men "who understood the times and knew what Israel should do." Apparently, they were the "wise men" on David's team. They took time to study everything that was going on around them and could declare with confidence to the people what they should do. These were the kind of men whom David needed and whom he relied on immensely during that particular time in Israel's history. If the men of Issachar were so effective even with the limited number of warriors they sent out, imagine the impact they could have had if they had sent more men.

The Bible makes another interesting mention of the tribe of Issachar in 1 Kings 15. During the time of the divided kingdom, we come across several kings who ruled in the northern kingdom and several in the southern kingdom. While some of them were good kings who feared God and did what was right in His sight, others did evil in His eyes. In this context we are told of a king of Israel named Nadab, son of Jeroboam. Nadab had no fear of God in his heart and instigated Israel to sin. While most of the people chose to ignore what was happening, one of the men of Issachar decided to do something about King Nadab:

> Baasha son of Ahijah from the tribe of Issachar plotted against him, and he struck him down at Gibbethon, a Philistine town, while Nadab and all Israel were besieging it. Baasha killed Nadab in the third year of Asa king of Judah and succeeded him as king.
>
> 1 Kings 15:27–28

Unable to stand the evil that Nadab was committing and appalled by his negative influence on the people, Baasha put an end to him and succeeded him as king. On assuming his new role, Baasha then went on to kill everyone from Jeroboam's family, because Jeroboam had done evil in the sight of God and had provoked God to anger. It seems Baasha was a man who detested evil, and he was provoked to anger by the things that provoked God. Somewhere along the way he changed, however, not for the better but for the worse. Baasha fell into the same sin as Jeroboam and began to walk in the same evil ways. This, in turn, incurred God's wrath and His harsh judgment against Baasha and his family:

> Then the word of the LORD came to Jehu son of Hanani concerning Baasha: "I lifted you up from the dust and appointed you ruler over my people Israel, but you followed the ways of Jeroboam and caused my people Israel to sin and to arouse my anger by their sins. So I am about to wipe out Baasha and his house, and I will make your house like that of Jeroboam son of Nebat. Dogs will eat those belonging to Baasha who die in the city, and birds will feed on those who die in the country."
>
> 1 Kings 16:1–4

The men of Issachar were given great potential and great wisdom. Many of them feared God and could not stand those who went against Him. Yet there were times when some of them failed by not making the best use of the opportunities that came their way. Even though they had been given the ability to understand the times, they did not always tap in to the potential God had given to them. They, too, fell in the way of sin and provoked God. In that way, Issachar and his tribe warn us that just because we have gifts and abilities, this does not mean that we will be successful in life, especially if we do not put them to good use.

Moses and the Tribe of Issachar

Moses speaks to the tribes of Zebulun and Issachar jointly, telling them more or less the same thing about their future. And like

Jacob, Moses also chooses to address Zebulun first, even though Issachar is older. Look at Moses' blessings on these tribes:

> Rejoice, Zebulun, in your going out, and you, Issachar, in your tents. They will summon peoples to the mountain and there offer the sacrifices of the righteous; they will feast on the abundance of the seas, on the treasures hidden in the sand.
>
> Deuteronomy 33:18–19

Or as *The Message* says,

> Celebrate, Zebulun, as you go out, and Issachar, as you stay home. They'll invite people to the Mountain and offer sacrifices of right worship, for they will have hauled riches in from the sea and gleaned treasures from the beaches.

Like the Zebulunites, the tribe of Issachar would also stand for what was right and would prosper exceedingly, both materially and spiritually. The only difference between these two is that the Zebulunites would rejoice in their going out, while the people of Issachar would rejoice in their tents. The future of the two tribes was similar, but it would unfold in different locations. The people of Issachar would not be straining themselves out at sea; they would relax within the confines of their tents. Yet Moses suggests that although Issachar's lot was within the tents, the tribe would share in the prosperity of Zebulun. There was abundance to be had both by land and by sea.

Today's Application for Us

What a rare combination we find in Issachar and later in his tribe— people who understood the times, yet sometimes lacked diligence; people who liked to escape from work and take it easy rather than making use of their God-given potential. It is a combination that should be rarer still according to Jacob's words, which were both a strong rebuke and a warning to Issachar and those like him.

It is important to be diligent in all we do; diligence brings the rewards of freedom and God's blessings. While rest is good and necessary, too much rest will make you rust! The Bible gives us some good examples of people whose diligence brought them God's rewards. Nehemiah was one. He served as cupbearer to King Artaxerxes, and some of his brethren returned from Judah to tell him that the city of Jerusalem was in ruins. On hearing this news, he was greatly troubled: "When I heard these things, I sat down and wept. For some days I mourned and fasted and prayed before the God of heaven" (Nehemiah 1:4).

Nehemiah requested that King Artaxerxes send him to rebuild the walls of Jerusalem. He had the favor of God and the king. The king not only consented to his request, but also sent his army officers and cavalry with him. After reaching Jerusalem and inspecting the ruins, Nehemiah informed the remnant of the Jews, the nobles, the priests and others of his desire: "Then I said to them, 'You see the trouble we are in: Jerusalem lies in ruins, and its gates have been burned with fire. Come, let us rebuild the wall of Jerusalem, and we will no longer be in disgrace'" (Nehemiah 2:17).

When some men in opposition, Sanballat, Tobiah and Geshem, heard about what Nehemiah and those with him were doing, they tried to dishearten them. These enemies mocked and ridiculed them, scheming and devising plans to hinder and delay the rebuilding of the wall (see Nehemiah 2:19). They tried hard to stop the work and even went to the extent of hiring Shemaiah to prophesy falsely to Nehemiah. But none of their plans to intimidate, frighten or trick Nehemiah into sinning succeeded. Nehemiah and the remnant of the Jews trusted God and prayed. God, in turn, frustrated the plans of their enemies (see Nehemiah 4:15).

Though the rebuilders of the wall were discouraged and made fun of, they never ceased working hard. Time and time again their enemies plotted to harm Nehemiah, but that did not slacken his efforts or deter him from completing the task of rebuilding Jerusalem's walls. The hard work and determination of Nehemiah and the remnant of the Jews paid off. Every step of the way, even as their persecution and challenges increased, Nehemiah and his people never gave up. Rather, they took their cares to the Lord and worked on diligently, so "the wall was completed on the twenty-fifth of Elul, in fifty-two days" (Nehemiah 6:15).

In the parable of the bags of gold in the New Testament, we read an example of the difference between those who are diligent and those who are not:

> Again, it will be like a man going on a journey, who called his servants and entrusted his wealth to them. To one he gave five bags of gold, to another two bags, and to another one bag, each according to his ability. Then he went on his journey. The man who had received five bags of gold went at once and put his money to work and gained five bags more. So also, the one with two bags of gold gained two more. But the man who had received one bag went off, dug a hole in the ground and hid his master's money.
>
> Matthew 25:14–18

Jesus continued this story by telling what happened when the master returned home. While the master was happy with the first two servants, who immediately worked hard and were able to double the money he had given them, he was angry with the third servant. Despite knowing that his master was a hard man, this third servant had not made use of the bag of money to try to increase it in any way. As a result, his master called him a wicked, lazy servant and gave his bag to one of the others. Jesus concluded, "For whoever has will be given more, and they will have an abundance. Whoever does not have, even what they have will be taken from them" (Matthew 25:29).

A detailed study of the apostle Paul's life reveals how he worked tirelessly in spreading the Gospel and how he traveled from place to place regardless of warnings and threats. His life was in constant danger. Undeterred, he worked hard and let nothing—not natural calamities like storms or shipwrecks, and not intentional attacks from bandits, Jews or Gentiles—discourage him or stop what he was doing.

Paul's passion shows in the fact that while he was in prison, he continued preaching and writing his epistles. Even while under house arrest in Rome for two years, he did not stop; he continued to preach the Gospel till the time he died. Paul made use of every opportunity to preach Christ. He portrays himself not just as an apostle, but also as a diligent worker:

> I have worked much harder, been in prison more frequently, been flogged more severely, and been exposed to death again and again. Five times I received from the Jews the forty lashes minus one. Three times I was beaten with rods, once I was pelted with stones, three times I was shipwrecked, I spent a night and a day in the open sea.
>
> 2 Corinthians 11:23–25

The list of things Paul faced and endured goes on. He and Barnabas ministered at Iconium, preaching to the Jews and Gentiles there. While many started to believe in Jesus, those who did not were enraged and plotted to kill these two preachers of the Gospel (see Acts 14:5). They fled to Lystra and Derbe, and in Lystra Paul again faced life-threatening opposition. After a lame man was healed, men from Antioch and Iconium stirred up trouble and they all took Paul outside the city and stoned him. He survived and went on to Derbe to minister (see verses 8–20).

The apostle Paul was immensely concerned about the Church. He strove constantly to encourage believers in numerous places and disciple them in the footsteps of Christ. Not only did he work hard in planting churches; he also made a conscious effort to visit and strengthen them time and again. After all the plots and stonings he suffered, he still returned to Lystra, Iconium and Antioch later: "They preached the gospel in that city [Derbe] and won a large number of disciples. Then they returned to Lystra, Iconium and Antioch" (Acts 14:21).

Truly, the apostle Paul is an exemplary example of absolute surrender and selfless service accompanied by immense hard work.

Whatever our situation, we need to follow his example and work diligently to fulfill the plan of God.

Nothing Could Stop Me

I remember that when I first started our church, I had only three people on the first day. We did not see any growth during those early days either. My dad had given me a bicycle as a gift, and I used to cycle thirty to forty kilometers a day, trying to meet people, talk to them about Jesus and invite them to church.

There were several days when I had no food to eat because there was no one in the church, and I literally was starving. I can recall receiving a letter from my mother that stated, "Paul, we heard that you are starving without food in Bangalore and that there is no one coming to the church. Please come back home. Dad and I will take care of you, and you can serve God along with us." But I never allowed anything to hold me back or prevent me from working hard in bringing souls into the Kingdom of God. I endured the days of hunger by spending a lot of time in prayer, and I worked hard every day to bring souls to Christ. In due course, the church started to grow.

I was a bachelor at that time, and I cannot think of a day when I stayed alone at home in my rented house and did nothing, just waiting for souls to show up at the church. My approach was different. I would go all by myself to different houses, one after the other, from morning to night, distributing tracts and sharing the Gospel of Jesus with the people. I still remember a day when I walked into a restaurant and did not have money even to order a cup of coffee. I drank water and continued cycling around to distribute tracts and share the Gospel.

I used to get severe asthma attacks during those days. I literally used to struggle in the nights to breathe, but I never allowed that to make me lazy in doing the work for which God had called me. In the meantime, God enabled me to buy a secondhand scooter from a fellow Christian minister. I remember one day when I went to visit a certain house and had only 5 rupees (about 34 cents) with me. I went to that house believing that I would get an offering after I had prayed for the family, but I got nothing. On the way back, I ran out of fuel and had to push my scooter all the way back to my house. It was raining, and I ended up having a severe asthma attack. It was so bad that when I reached home, I was soaking wet, struggling to breathe and unable even to put the scooter on its stand. I really thought I would die because I was totally breathless. But even at this crucial moment, I told God, *I will not allow this to stop me, but will work for You till You give me souls in the city of Bangalore.*

The local Assembly of God chairman came to my house one day and shouted at me for starving. Upset, he asked, "Why haven't you told me anything about your situation or visited my house for food?"

The only answer I could give him was, "Sir, if God has called me, let Him take care of me."

Hard labor and prayer have never let me down in the journey of my ministry. Even today, after 34 years, I believe in working hard for the Kingdom of God, for the Lord rewards our diligence.

Ways to Work Diligently for God

Issachar seemed to prefer rest to putting forth much effort working. That is not an example we want to follow. After much thought, I have identified a few qualities that I think lazy people share:

- They have potential and God-given opportunities, but they don't use them.
- They don't work hard.
- They envy other people's success.
- They grow comfortable and complacent.
- They indulge in self-pity.
- They are afraid of failure and the unknown.

- They procrastinate.
- They don't think for themselves; they prefer simply to do as they are told.
- They complain and give excuses for not doing what they should be doing.

Those are qualities we don't want to share. Neither did some of Issachar's tribe. Eventually, they rose above their forefather's lazy example and learned to stand and fight for what was right. Although the warriors among them were not great in number, they understood the times they lived in and knew what they should do in response. We can learn from them, and from the other examples we have seen in Scripture, that diligence brings with it the rewards and blessings of God. Along my way in ministry, I have learned a few factors that are essential in the life of anyone who desires to be diligent:

Absolute commitment is essential. We need to be committed to the task at hand. Unless we put our wholehearted effort into doing the task we are given, whatever we achieve will be less than our true potential. We may have the best knowledge and understanding of various situations, but our lack of commitment and laziness can destroy the entire potential God has given us. Many people who are highly educated have been unable to use that to progress in life. Commitment to do that which has to be done helps us achieve all our potential. Joshua reminded the people of Israel about all the miracles that God had done for them, right from the time of their forefathers Abraham, Isaac, Jacob, Moses and Aaron. He also made mention of what would happen if they went astray. As a result, the people said to Joshua, "We will serve the LORD our God and obey him" (Joshua 24:24).

Avoid distractions. Our total attention must be on the target or mission. We should not allow anything, no matter how attractive, to distract us. Focus is primary and essential. "Therefore, since we are surrounded by such a great cloud of witnesses, let us throw off everything that hinders and the sin that so easily entangles. And let us run with perseverance the race marked out for us, fixing our eyes on Jesus, the pioneer and perfecter of faith" (Hebrews 12:1–2). Even as we strive to achieve the task before us, Satan will attempt to hinder, delay or even stop our progress. Peter stepped out in faith and started walking on the water, with his eyes fixed on Jesus. But the second he paused to consider the things around him, he got distracted. When he shifted his focus away from Jesus, he started to sink (see Matthew 14:28–31). We need to avoid such distractions and stay highly focused.

Ask for God's help and anointing. We need God's help to complete the task set before us successfully. We need to ask Him for His help and anointing. That which we do through our own strength will never be as good as that which we do through God's help. The life of Jonah teaches us that when we try to do things through our own means, we end up paying the fare. We tend to rely on ourselves instead of relying on God and asking for His help. But when we trust God to take us to the destination, He will take care of everything. One mistake most of us make is that even when we ask God for help, we start comparing ourselves with others. When we make comparisons, we soon start drowning in the ocean of self-pity and disappointment, which finally leads us into depression. Instead of feeling incapable of doing what God has given us to do, we need to trust Him and work hard. We subconsciously undermine our potential when we rely on ourselves. We need to rely on and ask for God's help: "If any of you lacks wisdom, you should ask God, who gives generously to all without finding fault, and it will be given to you" (James 1:5).

Anticipate difficulties. Life is filled with challenges; we see new challenges knocking on our door almost every other day. We need to anticipate difficulties and be prepared to handle them. This requires that we be alert at all times. We cannot laze around, take things for granted and let go of valuable opportunities. A lot of people waste their God-given opportunities because of laziness, fear of the unknown and an unwillingness to anticipate or handle difficult situations. For example, many brilliant kids have parents who support them in going to a good college, but some of these kids don't make use of what God has given them because they are not able to cope with the challenges and difficulties they face. God gives us the opportunity to become men and women of great influence, but giving up in the face of difficulties kills that potential. "Watch out that you do not lose what we have worked for, but that you may be rewarded fully" (2 John 1:8).

Aim high—set a goal. We must have a target in mind, and the goal that we set, though high, must also be achievable. We must not become complacent. "The plans of the diligent lead to profit as surely as haste leads to poverty" (Proverbs 21:5). Never take a rest at the expense of your work. Even in the ministry, many men of God are unsuccessful because they feel that what they have is more than enough. One of the main reasons why churches don't grow is because some pastors feel satisfied with a smaller congregation, and they are unwilling to commit to larger responsibilities. They don't feel the need to grow a large church. They prefer a smaller congregation, even though their God-given capacity is large. We must aim big and work hard toward achieving our goal. Many people criticize megachurches, but they fail to understand the work that is behind such growth. The growth of a church depends on the vision of the pastor and the cooperation of the key leaders.

We must work hard to achieve great things for God. Though the task ahead seems impossible, we will be able to achieve it if we depend on God and use the talents He has given us, with the wisdom that comes from above. As Jesus told us, "What is impossible with man is possible with God" (Luke 18:27). Our commitment must be to the task ahead of us. Casting aside every distraction, we must succeed in doing the impossible!

Let's Pray Together

Loving heavenly Father, thank You for Your favor over our lives. We are so grateful that You walk with us each and every day and that we have Your Holy Spirit to guide us.

Give us the wisdom and focus to stay on the path You have made for us. Let Your supernatural strength and anointing rest on us. We know that many challenges lie ahead, but we choose to rely on Your grace to overcome them.

Do not allow us to grow comfortable or complacent in our current situation, as Issachar was, for we know that You have even greater plans for our lives than we can see or imagine. Bring them to pass as we work diligently for You.

In Jesus' name we pray, Amen.

7

Dan

Happy are those who are full of God,
for they will not allow anything
to come between Him and them.

During the initial stages of establishing our church, when it was
around four hundred people strong, a team from an international
organization came to visit us. They stayed with us for over a month
and did a study on our church. Pleased with what they saw, they
asked me to join their organization. They said they would make
me the head of their operations in India. Not only that, but they
also were willing to pay my wife and me separate salaries and even
give us a car and a house, which would have been a great luxury
at that time.

It was a tempting offer, but I did not let money or material possessions influence me. I knew the offer was not from God and turned it
down. I chose to stay with the Assemblies of God instead, a ministry
organization I have now been part of for over three decades. By the
grace of God, I have stayed faithful in the place God chose for me.

I have put Him first in every decision, and He has blessed me, my family and our ministries beyond measure.

It is vital not to let anything come between God and us. That is a powerful lesson we can learn from looking at the life of Dan and the Danites—a lesson they did not learn. There were others in Scripture, however, who learned it well. For example, in the book of Daniel, King Nebuchadnezzar asked the chief of his court officials to choose from among the exiles brought from Jerusalem young men who were "without any physical defect, handsome, showing aptitude for every kind of learning, well informed, quick to understand, and qualified to serve in the king's palace" (Daniel 1:4). Four young men, Daniel, Hananiah, Mishael and Azariah, were among those chosen for a three-year training program, after which they would enter the king's service. They were taught the Babylonian language and literature, and they were given special food and wine directly from the king's table. What an honor! But given the choicest food in the land, these four young men refused to partake of it because they did not want to defile themselves at the table of a heathen king. Though far away from their families and homes, and in spite of the temptations set before them, they made a strong decision in their hearts to stay true to God and kept themselves pure before Him. That is an example to follow!

Prophesying over his son Dan in Genesis 49, Jacob says he will be like a serpent, cunningly deceiving unsuspecting people and leading them astray. This comes true many years later as we see the Danites forgetting the God of their fathers, adapting to the ways of the heathen lands around them and alluring others into their wicked ways. In Deuteronomy 33 Moses had nothing of significance to say of this tribe either, a tribe that so easily forgot the God who was devoted to them. Here are a few verses that speak of the significance of putting God first in our lives, pleasing Him in all we do and letting nothing come between us:

You shall have no other gods before me.

Exodus 20:3

For the grace of God has appeared that offers salvation to all people. It teaches us to say "No" to ungodliness and worldly passions, and to live self-controlled, upright and godly lives in this present age.

Titus 2:11–12

Put to death, therefore, whatever belongs to your earthly nature: sexual immorality, impurity, lust, evil desires and greed, which is idolatry.

Colossians 3:5

I will be careful to lead a blameless life—when will you come to me? I will conduct the affairs of my house with blameless heart. I will not look with approval on anything that is vile.

Psalm 101:2–3

Rather, clothe yourselves with the Lord Jesus Christ, and do not think about how to gratify the desires of the flesh.

Romans 13:14

A life without God is a life with no meaning. Like a colorless rainbow, life without God is dull and drab; it contains no real love, joy or peace. As we trace the tragic history of Dan and the Danites, who drifted away from God and lost everything of true value in their lives, let us choose for ourselves to draw nearer to the One who is always there for us.

The Birth of Dan

Leah had given Jacob four children, Reuben, Simeon, Levi and Judah, while Rachel had remained barren. Unloved and ignored by Jacob, Leah suffered miserably. She depended greatly on God, however, sure of His presence in her life. She acknowledged His favor each time she gave birth to a child.

Rachel responded to her challenges rather differently. In her desperation, we see her going to her husband rather than crying out to God. Jealous because of the four children she saw around her sister, Leah, she was unable to take it anymore. She vented her anger and frustration on her husband, Jacob, and fought with him, crying out, "Give me children, or I'll die!" (Genesis 30:1). This stirred Jacob's anger, and in helplessness he retorted, "Am I in the place of God, who has kept you from having children?" (verse 2). His angry words seem to hint at blaming Rachel, since it was God Himself who had kept her from having children.

Not finding a solution, Rachel decided to take things into her own hands. She ran ahead of God and attempted to help Him fulfill His blessings on her life. She must have stormed out of the room after her fight with Jacob and dragged her maidservant, Bilhah, back with her. Pushing the other woman toward Jacob, without any hesitation Rachel told him, "Here is Bilhah, my servant. Sleep with her so that she can bear children for me and I too can build a family through her" (Genesis 30:3). This was a way that barren women of the time could gain children.

Eventually, Bilhah gave birth to a son. This brought tremendous joy to Rachel, who saw it as God standing up for her, even though her husband blamed her: "Then Rachel said, 'God has vindicated me; he has listened to my plea and given me a son.' Because of this she named him Dan" (Genesis 30:6). Though Dan's birth was a result of Rachel's manipulation, she chose to attribute it to God. To Rachel, the birth of Dan was a sign that God was on her side.

Much as with Zebulun and Issachar, however, the rest of Genesis mentions nothing of further significance about Dan. Other than being with the "sons of Jacob" whenever they were mentioned, Dan simply is listed in the record of those who went with Jacob to Egypt (see Genesis 46:23).

Jacob's Prophetic Words over Dan

Issachar was not the only one who might have been shocked and disappointed at what his father, Jacob, had declared over him.

Dan could have had the same reaction. Having spoken over the six sons borne by his wife Leah, Jacob now spots Dan, the first son borne by Rachel's maidservant, Bilhah. He had just compared Issachar to a donkey, and now he makes an even more startling animal comparison to Dan:

> Dan will provide justice for his people as one of the tribes of Israel. Dan will be a snake by the roadside, a viper along the path, that bites the horse's heels so that its rider tumbles backward.
>
> Genesis 49:16–17

The Message gives an interesting translation of this passage:

> Dan will handle matters of justice for his people; he will hold his own just fine among the tribes of Israel. Dan is only a small snake in the grass, a lethal serpent in ambush by the road when he strikes a horse in the heel, and brings its huge rider crashing down.

Jacob must have noticed as he watched Dan growing up that the boy had the good qualities of a judge. Dan probably could listen patiently to complaints and then convincingly deal with the issues. Sadly, his serpentlike qualities would override these good qualities. He would be crafty and deceiving, and he would strike unexpectedly. Although in Jacob's blessing Dan may have been small next to a horse, he had the ability to bring it down, along with its rider. He was also poisonous and would lie in wait to attack his prey.

This prophecy was indeed true about Dan, and his descendants would follow him in that course. The Danites had everything within them to live right, but they decided to live wrong. As we will see shortly, they knowingly defiled the God of Israel and rebelled against Him. And in their fall they pulled many others down with them.

Jacob feared that a day would come when Dan would develop disturbing, serpentlike qualities. Dreading all that might result, Jacob quickly breathed out a prayer: "I look for your deliverance, LORD" (Genesis 49:18). Or as *The Message* says, "I wait in hope for your salvation, GOD." Too shocked to believe the intensity of what he had spoken over Dan, Jacob turned to God for help and deliverance.

The Danites' Territory

Let's take a look at the descendants of Dan and how Jacob's words came to pass in their lives. After conquering the Promised Land, the first thing Joshua did was assign to each tribe the territory its people were to occupy. In the presence of God, he cast lots and distributed the land to the Israelites. During this distribution the Danites received their portion (see Joshua 18:1–10; 19:40–46). They seemed to be the only ones, however, who did not occupy the land God Himself had chosen to give them. Apparently, they found it too difficult. Acting on their willfulness instead—asking permission of neither God nor Joshua—they attacked a place called Leshem, destroyed its inhabitants and settled in it, renaming that place Dan (see Joshua 19:47).

The Danites gave up easily and failed to take hold of the land God had given them. By doing so, they lost a blessing that was rightfully theirs. Relying on their own strength, they moved away from the plan of God and lacked faith in what He could do for them. The book of Judges begins by listing all the tribes that failed to drive out the inhabitants in the territory assigned to them, in disobedience to what God had commanded in Deuteronomy 20:16–18. The Danites, of course, made that list. They had problems with the Amorites and only managed to suppress them by means of forced labor (see Judges 1:34–35). In Deborah's song, after Israel's victory over the Canaanites, she questions why the Danites shied away from the fight: "And Dan, why did he linger by the ships?" (Judges 5:17). The Danites seemed to loiter around while others were fighting to protect the land.

Because it was difficult, the Danites did not take the land God had given them. They let the difficulties come between Him and them. Neither did they drive out the Amorites, as God commanded. Nor did they join the fight against the Canaanites with Deborah and Barak; rather, they chose to loiter near the ships.

Clearly, the Danites were those who did not have a heart for God or the things of God. They had a problem setting their priorities straight. Above all, they lacked dependency on God. In fact, they seemed to have the very problems that we looked at in Samson in chapter 1, which is not surprising since Samson was also a Danite (see Judges 13).

The Danites' Sins against God

Instead of possessing their God-given land, the Danites wandered from place to place preying on innocent, vulnerable people who were unprepared to fight. At one point they sent five men to explore a certain land. On the way they stopped in the hill country of Ephraim and rested at the house of Micah, who had several silver images and idols set up and who also had hired a young Levite to serve him as priest in his house (see Judges 17–18). On meeting this Levite, the Danites implored him to ask God if the mission they were on would be successful. The young Levite assured them that they had God's approval. The five Danites then left Ephraim and came to Laish, whose people enjoyed safety, lacked nothing and were settled far away from other people. This seemed an ideal location, so the five reported back to their tribe. They stirred up the rest of the Danites to act against those innocent and unsuspecting people, saying that this was the land God was giving them.

The Danites sent six hundred men to capture Laish. On the way, the five Danites told their other brethren about Micah and his household gods, images and idols. Then they suggested, "Now you know what to do" (Judges 18:14). All of them together went to the house of Micah and took all the carved images, idols and household gods for themselves. On being questioned by the Levite, they tempted him to come along with them and be their priest, serving an entire tribe rather than just one family. Micah tried to stop them, but realized he was outnumbered and allowed them to leave.

This, then, is what the Danites did: First, they went to Laish to attack an unsuspecting people and burn the city to the ground. Then they went on to rebuild the city and name it Dan. They further set up all the idols and images they had taken from Micah so they could worship them, and they even had their own priests till the time of their captivity.

The Danites failed to walk in the ways of God. They knew He had chosen their people to be His own. They knew they should only worship Him and have no other gods besides Him. They knew they should not allow the heathen nations around them to pollute them. Yet in spite of all they knew, they chose to rebel against God in a detestable manner. Sadly, the Danites were the first tribe to bring idols into the Promised Land. They also influenced the rest of the tribes to go against the command of God in which He said, "You must not do as they do in Egypt, where you used to live, and you must not do as they do in the land of Canaan, where I am bringing you. Do not follow their practices" (Leviticus 18:3). The sinful mistake of the Danites led an entire generation away from God.

Later on in the history of Israel, when the kingdom was divided into two, we come across King Jeroboam. He feared that if his people went to Judah to worship God, they might be enticed to transfer their loyalty to Rehoboam, king of Judah. He therefore decided to set up two golden calves, one in Bethel and the other in Dan. He encouraged the people to worship these idols, saying, "Here are your gods, Israel, who brought you up out of Egypt" (1 Kings 12:28). In that way, once again the city of Dan became a place of idol worship.

The Danites did not even consider what they were doing as evil in the sight of God. Their hearts had become so callous that they made no effort to repent and turn back to Him. They absolutely displaced God from their lives. No wonder the prophet Amos said about them, "They will fall, never to rise again" (Amos 8:14). Probably the Danites' sins are the reason that while all Israel's other tribes are mentioned in the book of Revelation, including those of Reuben and Simeon, Dan is not mentioned at all (see Revelation 7:4–8). Dan stands for those who choose not to give God the right place in their lives, and in doing so stray far away from Him.

Moses and the Tribe of Dan

Although Moses had nothing much to say to the Danites, he prophetically speaks about them not settling in the land God had given them, but moving farther and farther away from it, into the north:

> Dan is a lion's cub, springing out of Bashan.
>
> Deuteronomy 33:22

The Message says almost the same thing:

> Dan is a lion's cub leaping out of Bashan.

By calling the Danites a lion's cub, Moses may be referring to their playful attitude and the fact that they did not take important matters seriously. He suggested that the Danites did not even take God seriously, settled in Bashan and drifted away from Him.

Amos probably had the Danites in mind when he addressed the people of Bashan and declared that God in His mercy waited for them to return to Him in repentance, but they did not do so. But God would wait no more; He would surely judge them (see Amos 4).

As I mentioned, Jacob himself was taken aback by the words he declared over Dan, and he looked to the Lord for deliverance. If only Dan had taken Jacob's words seriously and had instilled the fear of God in his descendants! Had Dan taught them to give God first priority, the future of the Danite tribe might have been different.

Today's Application for Us

Our future can be different if we learn the lesson Dan and the Danites teach us about not losing God's blessings. We cannot allow anything to come between us and the Lord. The consequences are too devastating. It is a lesson we also can learn from other scriptural examples, one of whom is Solomon. King Solomon was the wisest king who ever lived. He was the son of King David, and God chose him to take over the kingdom after David's death. The Bible tells us that the Lord loved Solomon (2 Samuel 12:24). We can see that Solomon reciprocated this love: "Solomon showed his love for the LORD by walking according to the instructions given him by his father David, except that he offered sacrifices and burned incense on the high places" (1 Kings 3:3). King David had a good relationship with God, but that did not mean King Solomon could take his own relationship with God for granted. Individually, he had to build and maintain that relationship by walking in the ways of God himself.

God favored Solomon and even told him to ask whatever he wanted from Him. While the natural instincts of a normal human being would drive someone to ask for riches, the comforts of this world or a life free from worries, Solomon was different. He desired something the world could not give him: "So give your servant a discerning heart to govern your people and to distinguish between right and wrong. For who is able to govern this great people of yours?" (1 Kings 3:9).

God was pleased that Solomon was not greedy for the riches of this world, but instead asked for wisdom. He not only gave Solomon the wisdom he asked for; He also gave him wealth and honor, to the extent that "King Solomon was greater in riches and wisdom than all the other kings of the earth" (1 Kings 10:23).

At first Solomon faithfully followed God and walked in accordance with His Word. But soon he allowed the things of this world to come between him and God and ruin the covenant God had made with him. It started with this: "King Solomon, however, loved many foreign women besides Pharaoh's daughter—Moabites, Ammonites, Edomites, Sidonians and Hittites" (1 Kings 11:1). Solomon's many foreign wives led him away from God. He even built high places for the foreign gods whom his wives worshiped, so that they could offer sacrifices and burn incense to them.

Despite his God-given wisdom, King Solomon failed to remember what God had commanded the children of Israel through Moses about the occupants of the land He was giving them. God had said,

> Do not intermarry with them. Do not give your daughters to their sons or take their daughters for your sons, for they will turn your children away from following me to serve other gods, and the LORD's anger will burn against you and will quickly destroy you.
>
> Deuteronomy 7:3–4

God's words served as a warning to His children to honor the words of the covenant and never wander away from it and so incur His wrath. King Solomon, being God's chosen one to lead the children of Israel, was supposed to be a godly model they could follow. He was destined to lead them in the ways of God, but instead, he allowed pagan religions and practices to adulterate the kingdom.

In the New Testament we see another example of what can happen when we allow anything to come between God and us. There is an interesting incident where a rich young man who felt he had kept all the commandments wanted to know how he could get eternal life. Here is what happened when he asked Jesus about it:

> Jesus answered, "If you want to be perfect, go, sell your possessions and give to the poor, and you will have treasure in heaven. Then come, follow me."
>
> When the young man heard this, he went away sad, because he had great wealth.
>
> Then Jesus said to his disciples, "Truly I tell you, it is hard for someone who is rich to enter the kingdom of heaven."
>
> Matthew 19:21–23

People are very attached to their wealth. Most often, they are willing to do anything as long as their wealth remains untouched or does not depreciate. This story shows us how the rich young man, though he followed all the commandments, allowed his wealth to come between him and God. People who live a life like this end up allowing the world to get into them.

The book of Acts chapter 4 narrates a time when the believers were united with one heart and mind. They shared their possessions, sold them when money was needed and helped the needy. A couple named Ananias and Sapphira sold a piece of their property and gave the money to the apostles. But they intentionally—and secretly—kept back part of the money for themselves. It was not that they had to give all the money; it was that they lied about it.

Peter asked the man, "Ananias, how is it that Satan has so filled your heart that you have lied to the Holy Spirit and have kept for yourself some of the money you received for the land?" (Acts 5:3). Sapphira lied about it as well, after her husband lied (see Acts 5:7–10).

Ananias and Sapphira acted deceptively. They had the wonderful opportunity of being a blessing to the Kingdom of God and being part of the early ministry of the apostles, but they allowed their love of money to come between them and God. As a result, this couple died.

Satan even tried to tempt Jesus by showing Him the kingdoms of the world and their riches. But Jesus resisted him and did not allow the riches of this world to take Him away from His God-ordained mission (see Matthew 4:8–10). He never allowed riches or anything else to come between Him and His Father.

Tempted by Prosperity

I decided right from the time I was in Bible college that my dependency would be on God and not man. I did not allow my parents to pay for my college studies. I had to cut grass and clean restrooms to pay my fees, but I was grateful that God provided me with the work. I stuck to my decision after college. I already mentioned that during the initial days of my ministry, there was a time when I did not have money even to buy one meal a day. One time when I had been starving for six days, I began to question God: *Did You really call me to do the ministry? Why do I have to struggle so much? Why are You allowing me to go through such a tough time?*

God answered by assuring me of His plan for my life, and He reminded me of the vision He had given me of having a large church in Bangalore. That answer revived me, and I started working in order to see God adding souls to His Kingdom. It was at this juncture that I received a letter from a foreign nation stating that a church there wanted me to come and be an associate pastor. They were willing to give me a house, a car and a generous salary. Imagine the temptation! Here I was without so much as an Indian rupee in my hand, starving and struggling to do ministry. Meanwhile, I had the option of allowing my desires to come between my God-given vision and me.

I want to draw your attention to something interesting. The invitation did not come at a point when I was thriving in the ministry. It came while I was struggling. Satan tempted Jesus at a time when He was hungry. The enemy tried to manipulate the situation by asking Him to turn the stones into bread (see Matthew 4:3). When I was at rock-bottom, Satan was trying to take away from me what God had intended for me by showing me a life of prosperity.

I knew the choice I had to make. I took the letter in my hand and . . . I tore it up and threw it out. I told God, *Even if I die, I will die for You in India, bringing souls into Your Kingdom.* That was my passion. I was unwilling to allow anything to come between God and me.

Ways to Stay Near to God

No matter how attractive something might seem, we must not allow it to come between God and us. It might momentarily draw our attention, but our spirit must always be inclined to God and alert to perceive what He actually desires of us. Those who make God the top priority in their lives will be:

- Inclined to God
- Inspired by God
- Inseparable from God

I have identified some steps that the Word of God teaches us to take that will prevent anything from coming between God and us: *Walk in obedience to God's Word*. The Word of God contains a wealth of wisdom. It has guidelines that can help us go through or handle any situation in life. The psalmist says those who stay close to Him "go from strength to strength, till each appears before God in Zion" (Psalm 84:7). The prophet Samuel tells Saul that "to obey is better than sacrifice" (1 Samuel 15:22). King Saul first disobeyed God by offering a sacrifice that he was not allowed to offer. Then he decided to do more things his own way. He ended up doing something God absolutely detested, which He had warned the children of Israel never to do: Saul consulted a medium (1 Samuel 28:3–25). The end result was that he damaged himself and also the people around him. We need to walk in obedience to God's Word and maintain a constant, consistent relationship with Him. The Bible says, "The righteous will flourish like a palm tree, they will grow like a cedar of Lebanon" (Psalm 92:12). That is the blessing we receive when we walk with God.

Wait on God. We need to cast our impatience aside and learn to wait on God. We get so accustomed to today's trend of everything being "instant" that we expect the same from God. God's ways are different. We need to wait in His presence. God speaks this through the prophet Isaiah: "Those who hope in the LORD will renew their strength. They will soar on wings like eagles; they will run and not grow weary, they will walk and not be faint" (Isaiah 40:31). The psalmist also encourages us, saying, "Wait for the LORD; be strong and take heart and wait for the LORD" (Psalm 27:14). We must not allow anything to break our spirit. We need to strengthen ourselves by waiting in His presence, for our strength comes not from man but from God.

Withdraw from worldly pleasures. It is important that we don't allow the pleasures of this world to take us away from God. The apostle Paul tells us, "As God has said: 'I will live with them and walk among them, and I will be their God, and they will be my people.' Therefore, 'Come out from them and be separate, says the Lord. Touch no unclean thing, and I will receive you'" (2 Corinthians 6:16–17). Isaiah 1:16 tells us, "Wash and make yourselves clean. Take your evil deeds out of my sight; stop doing wrong." We who are in God must always remember that our priority is to Him; He is the living God. People without that knowledge can worship something other than God and make it an idol above Him. We must identify such things and withdraw from them.

Watch our lives. Our lives are precious. The enemy is constantly prowling around trying to destroy us. The apostle Paul tells Timothy to watch his life so that no one will look down on him (see 1 Timothy 4:16). Jesus, too, told His disciples, "Watch and pray" (Matthew 26:41). The words of wisdom contained in the book of Proverbs teach us, "The highway of the upright avoids evil; those who guard their ways preserve their lives" (Proverbs 16:17). That is a truth we need to realize, because just being religious or having a rich spiritual heritage does not mean that we can take our spiritual life for granted. We have to live it out as our commitment to God. Things like spiritual pride, family and even ministry at times can come between God and us. We need to watch our lives carefully so this does not happen. We can never take our relationship with God for granted. Every individual is responsible for watching over his or her relationship with God.

War against the kingdom of darkness. The apostle Paul warns us about the warfare we will face (see Ephesians 6:11–12). While that can sound a little scary, we need not be afraid. God is with us, and He has given us the weapons we need to bring down the strongholds of the enemy. "The weapons we fight with are not the weapons of the world. On the contrary, they have divine power to demolish strongholds" (2 Corinthians 10:4). God does not mean for His children to be afraid or defeated. His plans are greater. We will be victorious only when we fight against the enemy with God's strength: "Therefore put on the full armor of God, so that when the day of evil comes, you may be able to stand your ground, and after you have done everything, to stand" (Ephesians 6:13).

We can never take our spirituality for granted. Our walk with God must be consistent so that we can protect ourselves from the enemy. The negative influence of this world is very strong. When God stopped speaking to Saul because he failed, Saul went to a medium to get instructions. This is the way in which Satan will damage our lives. We need to remain careful and alert. We cannot fight the enemy when we do not walk with God. Our walk must consist of waiting on God, walking in obedience to His Word and staying away from the distractions of this world. We must remain full of Him and never allow anything to come between us. Only then will we be victorious over the enemy and be successful in this life that God has given us.

Let's Pray Together

Our gracious heavenly Father, thank You that Your Son was the ultimate sacrifice for us. As we journey with You, fill us with Your wisdom so that we can overcome any obstacles that arise in our path. Allow us to see each challenge through Your eyes.

Remove impatience and our hunger for instant gratification from our minds. Teach us, Lord, to wait on You and seek Your perfect time. Guard us from the temptations of the world. Guide our steps and keep us from straying from

Your plan. Help us learn from the example of the Danites never to allow anything to separate us from You.

Sharpen our focus and tune our ears to the sound of Your voice. Equip us with strength and authority to overcome the enemy. Give us a fresh outpouring of Your grace.

In Jesus' name we pray, Amen.

8

Gad

Happy are those who trust and obey God,
for they will walk in victory
against their enemies.

As the church started growing, we began to think of shifting from our rental place to a place of our own. After much prayer, God miraculously gave us land in a central location in Bangalore. With a great deal of excitement we started planning the construction of our building at the site where the church now stands. The engineer who had to approve the building came to see the site but refused to grant us approval because he was expecting a huge amount of money as a bribe. Since the Word of God clearly denounces giving and taking bribes, I did not comply and offered him a soft drink and cake instead. The engineer did not budge, but told us to get a "no objection" certificate from the Forest Department to cut down a mango tree on our land. Then he left, thinking the task he had given us would be impossible. (According to our government's Tree Protection Act, the cutting of mango trees, even on private land, is not permitted.)

As I stood there praying and wondering how to proceed, my secretary came up and told me that a man had come to see me for prayer. This man had some problem with his fingers and was in terrible pain. I prayed for God to do a miracle. Two days later he came back completely healed. He was happy and asked me if there was anything he could do to help me. Imagine my astonishment when he told me he was a forest officer! We got permission to cut down the tree in no time, and I went to see the engineer, but he still refused to approve the construction.

I went home and fasted and prayed for ten days. I then went to his office, placed my hand on his name board and prayed that he would not be a hindrance to God's work. In just three hours' time he was dismissed from his position. His deputy took over and approved the construction immediately, overjoyed that his first act at work was to sanction the building of a church. I held on to God in spite of adverse circumstances, and He honored my trust in Him and came through, giving us the victory.

First Samuel 17 records David's confrontation with Goliath the giant. Standing tall above the rest of the soldiers around him, Goliath challenged any brave Israelite soldier to come out and fight him one-on-one, but no one dared. As the terrified Israelites looked on, David, a young shepherd boy with the anointing of God on him, stepped forward. His words revealed his confidence and absolute trust in the living God. He told Goliath, "This day the LORD will deliver you into my hands . . . and the whole world will know that there is a God in Israel. . . . The LORD saves; for the battle is the LORD's, and he will give all of you into our hands" (1 Samuel 17:46–47). God honored David's trust. As the stone flew out from David's sling and hit Goliath, the giant fell facedown, lifeless (see verses 49–51).

Trust in God brings victory in our battles. Jacob's last words to his son Gad in Genesis 49 are few, but significant. He says Gad will be attacked but will fight back valiantly. In Deuteronomy 33 Moses conveys this same message about the Gadites. He blesses them as a warrior tribe who will readily fight the battles that come their way with God on their side and return victorious. Here are a few verses from the Bible that tell us how essential it is to trust in the Lord in every situation:

> But blessed is the one who trusts in the LORD, whose confidence is in him. They will be like a tree planted by the water that sends out its roots by the stream. It does not fear when heat comes; its leaves are always green. It has no worries in a year of drought and never fails to bear fruit.
>
> Jeremiah 17:7–8

> When I am afraid, I put my trust in you. In God, whose word I praise—in God I trust and am not afraid. What can mere mortals do to me?
>
> Psalm 56:3–4

> When you pass through the waters, I will be with you; and when you pass through the rivers, they will not sweep over you. When you walk through the fire, you will not be burned; the flames will not set you ablaze.
>
> Isaiah 43:2

> I put no trust in my bow, my sword does not bring me victory; but you give us victory over our enemies, you put our adversaries to shame. In God we make our boast all day long, and we will praise your name forever.
>
> Psalm 44:6–8

> When you go to war against your enemies and see horses and chariots and an army greater than yours, do not be afraid of them, because the LORD your God, who brought you up out of Egypt, will be with you.
>
> Deuteronomy 20:1

As we read about Gad and the triumphs of the Gadites and realize that it was only because of God that they succeeded, let's place our hands in the powerful hands of our Master and walk in victory with Him.

The Birth of Gad

Desperate to have a family of her own, Rachel had given her maid-servant to Jacob to bear children for her. Soon her sister, Leah, realized that she had stopped bearing children. What did she do? Did she depend on God, as she had done several times in the past, or did she choose to act on her own will?

Most of us would suppose that Leah chose to cry out to God and ask Him to favor her again, but sadly, influenced by what Rachel had done, she decided to do what she felt best. Like Rachel, she took her maidservant, Zilpah, and gave her to Jacob as well (see Genesis 30:9). Leah probably did this to show Rachel that the struggle between the two of them had not come to an end, and that she would continue to have even more children than Rachel.

By this time Rachel's maidservant had given birth to two sons, Dan and Naphtali. This would have brought great joy to Rachel, who now had children to care for. This must have made Leah envious of her sister, with the result that she, too, gave Jacob her maidservant. "Leah's servant Zilpah bore Jacob a son. Then Leah said, 'What good fortune!' So she named him Gad" (Genesis 30:10–11).

The footnote in my Bible clarifies that Leah actually may have said, "A troop is coming," because the name Gad could mean either "good fortune" or "a troop." Either meaning applies well to Leah's situation. She may have regarded Gad's birth as a sheer stroke of luck and so may have exclaimed, "How lucky I am!" On the other hand, since Leah already had four sons of her own and now a fifth was added through Zilpah, she could have declared that she soon would have a crowd of children around her. Imagine her looking at Rachel and saying, "There are more to come. I will soon have a troop!" With the birth of Gad, Leah supposed that she had an edge over Rachel.

Like many of the other sons of Jacob, Gad is only once mentioned by name in the rest of Genesis, although there is one stray incident that refers to him in passing. Early in the narration of Joseph's story, we read that one time Joseph "was tending the flocks with his brothers, the sons of Bilhah and the sons of Zilpah, his father's wives, and he brought their father a bad report about them" (Genesis 37:2). Gad would have been among those sons of Zilpah, and something those young men said or did made Joseph feel the necessity of letting his father know about it. Besides that one incident, Gad is mentioned only in the list of people who migrated to Egypt with Jacob (see Genesis 46:16).

Jacob's Prophetic Words over Gad

After speaking words that prophetically foresaw his son Dan causing people's downfall with his serpentlike qualities, Jacob next addresses Gad, the first son born to Zilpah, Leah's maidservant:

> Gad will be attacked by a band of raiders, but he will attack them at their heels.
>
> Genesis 49:19

In *The Message* Jacob's words read,

> Gad will be attacked by bandits, but he will trip them up.

It is amazing how Jacob, whom God had touched and transformed at Bethel, is so aligned to the Spirit of God that the words he declared over his sons were all fulfilled many years later, even through their descendants. The son whom Jacob now saw by his bedside may not have looked anything like a warrior, yet Jacob saw in Gad a bold fighter.

After hearing all that Jacob had said to his brothers before him, Gad must have wondered what his father would say to him. His face must have fallen as he heard his father declare that he would be attacked by raiders. That did not sound promising at all, but then Gad realized that Jacob was still speaking about him.

When Gad heard his father's remaining words, what joy must have filled him. These were promising words indeed! Gad would put his attackers to flight. Though many might come against him, Gad would stand and fight without giving up.

The Gadites' Inheritance

Let's look at the fulfillment of Jacob's prophecy many years later, in Gad's descendants. The Gadites and the Reubenites observed that the land on the Transjordan side, east of the Jordan, was more suitable for them than on the other side since they had such large herds and flocks. They did not want to cross over the Jordan. They went to Moses, Eleazar and the rest of the leaders of Israel and expressed a desire to settle in Gilead, on the east side of the river.

This request angered Moses, who recollected how the report of the ten spies had disheartened the people and they had refused to take the Promised Land. Moses questioned these two tribes: "Should your fellow Israelites go to war while you sit here? Why do you discourage the Israelites from crossing over into the land the LORD has given them?" (Numbers 32:6–7).

These tribes quickly replied,

> We would like to build pens here for our livestock and cities for our women and children. But we will arm ourselves for battle and go ahead of the Israelites until we have brought them to their place. . . . We will not return to our homes until each of the Israelites has received their inheritance.
>
> Numbers 32:16–18

Moses was pleased with their suggestion. He told them that as long as they kept their word and crossed over the Jordan to assist their brothers in possessing the land, they could then return to their homes, free from any obligation to the Lord or to the rest of the Israelites.

Along with the Reubenites and the half-tribe of Manasseh, the Gadites did keep their word to Moses. Nearly forty thousand men from these tribes crossed over to assist their brother tribes (see

Joshua 4:12–13). After the Israelites had taken possession of the Promised Land and settled in it, Joshua called these tribes together, commended their commitment to Moses, said he appreciated their obedience and released them to return to their homes on the other side of the Jordan. He encouraged them to keep the Law, to love God, to walk in His ways and to hold fast to Him. Having received Joshua's blessings, the Gadites, the Reubenites and the half-tribe of Manasseh returned to their homes (see Joshua 22:1–9).

The Monument of the Gadites

While returning to their homes, the Gadites, the Reubenites and the half-tribe of Manasseh feared that a day would come when the Jordan would come between them and the other tribes. They dreaded that this would result in their future generations failing to fear the Lord. With good intentions, they built an altar by the Jordan in an attempt to prevent this.

When the other tribes heard about what they had done, they got ready to go to war against them (see Joshua 22:10–12). Phinehas and the other leaders of Israel went to Gilead to accost these "rebellious" tribes, asking them, "How could you break faith with the God of Israel like this? How could you turn away from the LORD and build yourselves an altar in rebellion against him now?" (Joshua 22:16).

We see the humility and wisdom with which the Gadites and their brethren diffused this volatile situation. They were quick to express their allegiance to the God of Israel, the Mighty One, and clarify that they had not rebelled against Him. They explained that they had built the altar to ensure that their future generations were not disregarded by the descendants of those tribes who had settled on the opposite side of Jordan. The altar simply was meant to stand as a monument of the Israelites' unity; that was its sole purpose. When Phinehas and the rest heard their explanation, they were pleased (see Joshua 22:26–31).

The Gadites were a great help to their fellow Israelites. They not only helped them fight their enemies and take possession of their land, but during times of great threat, people from the other tribes came to them for refuge. During the time of King Saul, when the Philistines attacked the Israelites, many of the Israelites came to the land of the Gadites and were safe there (see 1 Samuel 13:5–7). The Gadites stand out as a selfless people who did not hesitate to help their brothers.

The Gadites and King David

The Gadites who joined David in an endeavor to make him king of Israel were described this way: "They were brave warriors, ready for battle and able to handle the shield and spear. Their faces were the faces of lions, and they were as swift as gazelles in the mountains" (1 Chronicles 12:8). Among them were men who did not allow the overflowing Jordan to terrorize them, but rather chose to cross those waters and come to David's aid. They are further described this way:

> These Gadites were army commanders; the least was a match for a hundred, and the greatest for a thousand. It was they who crossed the Jordan in the first month when it was overflowing all its banks, and they put to flight everyone living in the valleys, to the east and to the west.
>
> 1 Chronicles 12:14–15

The courageous Gadites were "able-bodied men who could handle shield and sword, who could use a bow, and who were trained for battle" (1 Chronicles 5:18). They were also described as men "armed with every type of weapon" (1 Chronicles 12:37). As determined as a lion is to get its prey, so also were these Gadites set to defeat their enemies. They were quick-footed and easily gave their enemy the slip. Such warriors were the Gadites that people were afraid of them!

138

An interesting thing about the Gadites is that although they were well trained, strong and fearless, they did not rely on their own strength and abilities. In humility they chose to trust God. We are told that when they fought the Hagrites, God helped them and gave them victory. The Bible tells us exactly why: "They were helped in fighting them, and God delivered the Hagrites and all their allies into their hands, because they cried out to him during the battle. He answered their prayers, because they trusted in him" (1 Chronicles 5:20).

Although their position by the Jordan made them an easy target for the enemy, the Gadites never grew weary of fighting. When the Assyrians attacked Israel, the Gadites, the Reubenites and the half-tribe of Manasseh were the first to be carried into captivity (see 2 Kings 15:29; 1 Chronicles 5:26).

Moses and the Tribe of Gad

In his prophetic words over the tribes of Israel, Moses had much to say about the Gadites:

> Blessed is he who enlarges Gad's domain! Gad lives there like a lion, tearing at arm or head. He chose the best land for himself; the leader's portion was kept for him. When the heads of the people assembled, he carried out the LORD's righteous will, and his judgments concerning Israel.
>
> Deuteronomy 33:20–21

In *The Message* we read,

> Blessed is he who makes Gad large. Gad roams like a lion, tears off an arm, rips open a skull. He took one look and grabbed the best place for himself, the portion just made for someone in charge. He took his place at the head, carried out GOD's right ways and his rules for life in Israel.

Moses commends the Gadites' ability to fight like a lion, striking hard at their enemies. His prophecy proves accurate in every detail, since as we saw already, the Gadites were described during the time of David as men with faces like lions. Moses also refers to the fact that the Gadites chose the best land for themselves, land that seemed just right for someone in charge. He probably refers to the incident where the leaders of Israel gathered together at Gilead when the Gadites, Reubenites and half the tribe of Manasseh had built a monument. It was the Gadites who rose to the occasion and peacefully settled the issue.

Moses rejoices that God chose to make Gad's domain large. They were the ones who called on God, put their trust in Him and went out to fight valiantly. In doing so, the God they projected to others was a big God. The Gadites were indeed blessed for showing others, especially the heathen nations, how mighty their God was.

Today's Application for Us

God never fails the people who trust in Him. He proved to the people of Israel time and again that He would fight for them and give them the victory, if only they would trust Him and obey His commandments. The biblical account of the life of King Jehoshaphat, a king of Judah, is one example of this. It reveals to us the immense trust that this king and the people of Israel had in God. During Jehoshaphat's reign the Moabites, Ammonites and Meunites joined together, forming a vast army that came to attack Judah. When King Jehoshaphat heard of this, of course he was alarmed. But look at his first response: "Jehoshaphat resolved to inquire of the LORD, and he proclaimed a fast for all Judah. The people of Judah came together to seek help from the LORD; indeed, they came from every town in Judah to seek him" (2 Chronicles 20:3–4).

Once the people had assembled, King Jehoshaphat stood up in their midst and began to pray. He declared the sovereign Lordship of the Almighty God and reminded the people of how God had made a covenant with them. He also reminded God of how He had not allowed the children of Israel to invade the territory of the people of Ammon, Moab and Mount Seir, whereas here these people were, coming to try to take possession of the land that God had given the Israelites as their inheritance. Jehoshaphat prayed an honest, open prayer: "Our God, will you not judge them? For we have no power to face this vast army that is attacking us. We do not know what to do, but our eyes are on you" (2 Chronicles 20:12). God assured His people that He would fight for them and be their Deliverer (see verses 14–17). On hearing that, the people began to praise God. Even as they were going out to fight they were praising God, and He set an ambush and turned the three attacking nations against each other so that they destroyed themselves. When the people of Judah arrived on the scene, they found only the dead bodies of their attackers. The children of Israel had not given up, even though the threat they faced was extreme. They had depended on God, and God had not failed them. He had fought for them and given them the victory.

Jesus' words in a time of despair, when a synagogue leader's young daughter had just died, help us understand what God wants us to do at all times—trust in Him. Overhearing and ignoring what those who brought the terrible news of her death said, Jesus told Jairus, the synagogue ruler, "Don't be afraid; just believe" (Mark 5:36). Then He restored the girl to her parents—alive. On another occasion, Jesus said, "With man this is impossible, but with God all things are possible" (Matthew 19:26). Jesus instructs us to trust Him regardless of the circumstances, for there is nothing that God cannot do.

The Bible tells us about the ministry of Paul and Silas and their trust in God. From their example we can see again that trust brings victory. One time they were falsely accused of causing chaos and confusion in the city of Philippi. They were publicly stripped, flogged and thrown into prison, where they were put in chains and kept in a cell. A normal man's reaction in a situation like that would differ from how these two reacted. A normal man probably would have become dejected, disappointed and depressed, asking God why all this was happening to him. Not Paul and Silas. A situation like that did not deter them from praising God. The

Bible says that at midnight, instead of sleeping they were singing hymns and praying, and all the prisoners could hear them. "Suddenly there was such a violent earthquake that the foundations of the prison were shaken. At once all the prison doors flew open, and everybody's chains came loose" (Acts 16:26).

God not only set them free when they praised Him, but also loosened the chains of the other prisoners. Paul and Silas did not give up or let the circumstances weigh down their spirits. Rather, even in the midst of trials and tribulation they trusted God and kept praising Him, and He set them free.

Trusting God in Every Step

During the time when we were about to shift our church from the rental building into our own place, some people tried to get a stay order so that we would not be able to hold services in our new building. Basically, this was because we had constructed the church in a residential area. We found out about the stay order because a friend of one of my associate pastors had gone to a shop to have his résumé typed out. While he was there, he saw that the person in the shop was typing out another document. He glanced at it and happened to see my name in several places. My associate pastor had mentioned my name to this friend on several occasions, so the man recognized it and decided to find out what the document was all about. He read it while the person was typing it out. In that way, this man found out that some people were trying to get a stay order against our church building. He immediately dropped the documents he was carrying and rushed to tell my associate pastor about what he had discovered.

As soon as I heard what was happening, the Spirit of God gave me the wisdom to shift the church immediately to our own place. We moved everything out of the rental building into our half-constructed church building. We further informed all our congregation members that our service that Sunday would be in the basement of the new building. In that situation, God gave us the victory. The people failed in getting a stay order because we had already taken possession of the new building. Further, since it was in the part of a defense area that was a residential section for retired army officers, there was a provision for a worship center to be built there, and our church was registered as the Full Gospel Assembly of God Worship Center. We trusted God in every step we took, and He fought all our battles.

On another occasion, some people sent an accusatory letter against me to the higher authorities. Following that, some officers with handcuffs came to the church office to arrest me. Even in that situation, the Lord was with me and granted me favor. I told the officers that I would come and meet with the police commissioner the next day, because we were just getting ready for the dedication of the basement. The officers then left, and I kept praying that whole night. I did not give up. The next morning, with two elderly and influential people from the church, I went to meet with the commissioner, as I had said I would do.

On seeing me, the commissioner offered me some coffee and asked, "Would you like to see the names of those who have sent the accusation letter?"

I replied, "I don't want to see it. Let God see it! In due time, He will justify everything."

Hearing my response, the police commissioner said, "This itself is proof that you are trusting God and that you don't want to take any revenge on those people! Your church is growing large, and you are now popular. Many are upset and jealous about your growth. I am canceling this case."

He closed the file and added that they would not take in any more accusations against me. Trust in God had brought me victory.

Ways to See Victory through Trust

Through all my experiences and through what we have seen from the Bible about Gad and the Gadites, God taught me five important lessons about the blessings of God that come with trust:

Give glory to God, realizing that He is the One who fights our battles. The psalmist encourages us, saying, "Among the gods there is none like you, LORD; no deeds can compare with yours. All the nations you have made will come and worship before you, LORD; they will bring glory to your name" (Psalm 86:8–9). Battles fought with human strength will only result in defeat, while battles fought with the strength of God will surely result in victory. Moses tells the children of Israel, "The LORD will fight for you; you need only to be still" (Exodus 14:14). While we give God the glory, this is the assurance that God gives us.

Grace is the foundation of our trust in God. Our ability to have faith and trust in God springs from His grace upon our lives. "For it is by grace you have been saved, through faith—and this is not from yourselves, it is the gift of God" (Ephesians 2:8). The apostle Paul says, "He has saved us and called us to a holy life—not because of anything we have done but because of his own purpose and grace. This grace was given us in Christ Jesus before the beginning of time" (2 Timothy 1:9).

Guard ourselves from retaliating in the flesh. It becomes easy for us to act in the flesh and retaliate. That brings no blessings! "Do not take revenge, my dear friends, but leave room for God's wrath, for it is written: 'It is mine to avenge; I will repay,' says the LORD" (Romans 12:19). In the Sermon on the Mount, Jesus said, "Blessed are you when people insult you, persecute you and falsely say all kinds of evil against you because of me. Rejoice and be glad, because great is your reward in heaven" (Matthew 5:11–12).

Grow in the wisdom and the anointing of the Holy Spirit to discern between spiritual and physical attacks. True ability to discern between a spiritual and physical attack becomes possible only when we are filled with the Holy Spirit and the Word of God. "But solid food is for the mature, who by constant use have trained themselves to distinguish good from evil" (Hebrews 5:14). Our prayer must be, "Teach me knowledge and good judgment, for I trust your commands" (Psalm 119:66).

Gear up *for the victory God has set before us.* We need to cheer up and never give up because "victory rests with the LORD" (Proverbs 21:31). The victory that God has prepared for us belongs to us. Bearing in mind that He has already promised to give us the victory, we need to move forward confidently. "But thanks be to God, who always leads us as captives in Christ's triumphal procession and uses us to spread the aroma of the knowledge of him everywhere" (2 Corinthians 2:14).

We need to live in realization of the fact that while we face an earthly battle, we also face a spiritual battle. But the good news is that God has not only assured us of His constant presence, but also has won the victory for us. Hence, we need to march forward and take possession of that which God has given us. When we trust and obey Him, He brings us the blessings of victory.

Let's Pray Together

Gracious heavenly Father, You are our strength and our righteousness. You protect us and lead us to victory during battle, as You led the Gadites. When our situation seems impossible, we know we can trust You to deliver us.

Your gift of grace is the cornerstone of our faith. Thank You for loving us even though we are undeserving. Grant us patience in trying times, so that we do not retaliate in haste.

We resolve to meditate on Your wisdom and move only when the Holy Spirit leads us. We will hold fast to Your promises and proclaim victory in every area of our lives.

In Jesus' name we pray, Amen.

9

Asher

Happy are those who know
who their God is, for they will enjoy
prosperity and protection.

I recollect an incident that happened when the construction work
on our church was in progress. My associate pastor in charge of
the church's accounts told me one day that the cement supplier
had refused to deliver any more bags of cement since we had not
paid him the amount we owed him. We had no funds in our hands
right then, and we had only Indian rupees 700 in the bank ($46.67
at that time). As I was praying and looking to God, the Lord gave
me the faith to write a check for Indian rupees 40,000 ($2,667).
I wrote a check for that amount and handed it to my associate
pastor to give to the cement supplier.

Aware of the meager amount we had in the bank, my associate
pastor asked me, "What do we do if the check bounces, Pastor?"

I replied, "A faith check will never bounce! The Lord is our
provider."

The cement supplier received the check and happily gave us one
hundred more bags of cement, but I knew the battle was yet to be

won. I went down to our church basement, where our office was located back then, and I started to pray. I told my secretary that I did not want to meet with anyone that day, as I had to pray and receive the miracle God had prepared for us.

After a few hours, my secretary told me that a family had come to see me. Since I was in prayer, I asked her to take them to one of my associate pastors. She came back after a few minutes and said they were adamant that they wanted to meet no one but me. Left with little choice, I asked her to send them to me. When I met them, they said they wanted to receive salvation. I taught them quickly and briefly from the Word of God, and I prayed with them.

Overjoyed in their newfound faith, this family thanked me and gave me an offering in an envelope. When I opened the envelope, inside was a check for exactly Indian rupees 40,000. What a miracle! We were able to pay the cement supplier that day because of our unshakable confidence in our God, who would never let us down.

Note that I am not suggesting in this story that Christians should routinely write checks by faith that they cannot cover. Unless guided by the Holy Spirit, one should not try to imitate another person's faith steps. In obedience to the word of the prophet, the leper Naaman went and dipped himself in the river Jordan and was cleansed immediately. But that does not mean that every leper who dips himself in any river will be cleansed—unless he or she receives a specific word from God to do so.

I remember a similar incident when we had no money to go ahead with our construction. As the workers waited for me to tell them what to do, I walked in front of the building and prayed for a miracle. I trusted in God alone to take us through this situation. Just then, a man walked up and handed me an offering of Indian rupees 10,000 ($667). God had told him on the previous day to give me the offering, and he apologized to me for the delay. Thanking God in my heart, I accepted the offering and very kindly told him that the next time God told him to do something, he ought to do it immediately. God did a miracle yet again, and we were able to continue with the construction.

God's providence is always available to us in our times of need as we rely entirely on Him. We will see from our look at Asher and his descendants that it is those who know who their God is who will enjoy His provision and protection. In Genesis 49 Jacob prophesies over his son Asher prosperity and a land filled with bounty. Later, Moses' blessing echoes Jacob's words as he blesses the tribe of Asher in Deuteronomy 33 with favor, strength, abundance and God's protection. As the men of Asher dwelt in their God-given land, these words of God came true in their lives.

Being confident in who our God is brings with it many blessings. In Numbers 13 Moses sends twelve Israelite men to spy out the land of Canaan before the Israelites advance in battle to possess the Promised Land. Ten spies come back and spread fear in the camp, saying there are giants in the land whom the Israelites will never be able to prevail against. These ten spies and those who listened to their report were forgetting all the miracles God already had worked among them.

Caleb, however, one of the two remaining spies, speaks out boldly, with faith in the God of Israel. He says, "We should go up and take possession of the land, for we can certainly do it" (Numbers 13:30).

The people did not listen to Caleb or Joshua (the other spy who brought a good report), and it would be forty long years before Joshua finally was able to lead them in their conquest of the Promised Land (see Joshua 5:6). By then Caleb had reached the age of 85, but that did not stop him. His confidence in the Lord was stronger than ever. He waged war against the giant people of the Anakites and inherited Hebron "because he followed the LORD, the God of Israel, wholeheartedly" (Joshua 14:14). Here are a few more Bible verses that speak of the blessings of those who are confident in who God is:

This is what the LORD says: "Let not the wise boast of their wisdom or the strong boast of their strength or the rich boast of their riches, but let the one who boasts boast about this: that they have the understanding to know me, that I am the LORD, who exercises kindness, justice and righteousness on earth, for in these I delight," declares the LORD.

Jeremiah 9:23–24

I put no trust in my bow, my sword does not bring me victory; but you give us victory over our enemies, you put our adversaries to shame. In God we make our boast all day long, and we will praise your name forever.

Psalm 44:6–8

The people that do know their God shall be strong, and do exploits.

Daniel 11:32 KJV

You, LORD, keep my lamp burning; my God turns my darkness into light. With your help I can advance against a troop; with my God I can scale a wall.

Psalm 18:28–29

I know whom I have believed, and am convinced that he is able to guard what I have entrusted to him until that day.

2 Timothy 1:12

As we read about Asher, the Asherites and some others in the Bible who lived confidently depending on God and enjoying His blessings, let's be encouraged to rest in the Lord as He accompanies us through life's long journey.

The Birth of Asher

We saw in the previous chapter how Leah had declared herself fortunate when her maidservant, Zilpah, gave birth to Gad. Leah saw that God was enlarging her family, adding son after son to her. No doubt she guessed that this would trouble her sister, Rachel, who up to that time had borne no sons of her own. Leah took delight in the fact that although she may have failed in getting her husband, Jacob, to love her, she now had many sons on whom she could shower her love and attention.

After giving birth to Gad, Leah's maidservant had yet another boy: "Leah's servant Zilpah bore Jacob a second son. Then Leah said, 'How happy I am! The women will call me happy.' So she named him Asher" (Genesis 30:12–13). On seeing another son, Leah was indeed happy. She considered herself blessed to have not one, not two, but six sons, while her sister only had two, neither of which she had given birth to herself (they were her maidservant's).

Leah had mainly focused on God as the One who saw her difficult situation, heard her cry and favored her by blessing her with children. When it came to the sons borne by Zilpah, however, Leah focused more on herself. After Gad's birth her exclamation was, "What good fortune!" And on the birth of Asher she proclaimed, "How happy I am!" Both of these times it was all about her, not about her husband and not even about God. Asher's birth made Leah swell with pride. She knew that all the women around her, including Rachel, would see her six sons and realize how happy she must be.

Aside from the record of his birth, Asher is not mentioned specifically by name again in most of the other events of Genesis. Like many of his brothers, Asher played no significant role other than being present in "the sons of Jacob" passages. We do find his name once more, however, in the list of those who moved to Egypt with Jacob (see Genesis 46:17).

Jacob's Prophetic Words over Asher

After Jacob had spoken over Gad, describing him as a great warrior who would put his enemies to flight, he spotted Gad's full brother, Asher. They had been born of the same mother, Zilpah. Jacob spoke this over Asher's life:

Asher's food will be rich; he will provide delicacies fit for a king.

Genesis 49:20

The same prophecy in *The Message* reads,

Asher will become famous for rich foods, candies and sweets fit
for kings.

Although Jacob spoke very little over Asher, his words were of
great substance. In essence, he was declaring abundant material
prosperity on Asher and his sons. Asher would prosper to such an
extent that he would stand before kings. Not only would Asher
eat rich food, but he would also serve rich delicacies to others,
especially to kings. Let's look at how some of that richness came
to pass in the life of Asher's descendants.

The Asherites in the Old Testament

The Asherites were not flawless; they made some mistakes and
wrong choices. But when their flaws were brought to their attention, they were quick to take note and, though it was difficult, make
the necessary changes. For example, the Asherites were among the
tribes that disobeyed God and failed to drive out the Canaanites
from the land God had given them (see Judges 1:31–32). They
further did not care to respond to the call of Deborah and Barak
when the need arose for all the tribes to join hands in fighting the
Canaanites. The judge Deborah says of them in her song, "Asher
remained on the coast and stayed in his coves" (Judges 5:17). Those
from Asher shied away from their responsibility at the time. They
chose rather to remain at home, by the seacoast (see Joshua 19:24–
31). Not wanting to take a risk, they preferred the security of their
own harbors. What a shame that when many of the other tribes
joined together to fight, the Asherites looked to their own safety.

Probably spurred on by Deborah's words, the Asherites later
did respond to a call to fight. When Gideon sent messengers

calling for men from Manasseh, Asher, Zebulun and Naphtali to help him fight the Midianites, the Asherite warriors rose to the occasion and joined in the battle. They were among those who pursued the Midianites (see Judges 6:35; 7:23). What a drastic change—from men who hesitated to fight, to men who came out of their comfort zone and fought alongside their brothers. These Asherite warriors were described as "choice men, brave warriors and outstanding leaders" (1 Chronicles 7:40). Or as *The Message* words it, "These were Asher's sons, all of them responsible, excellent in character, and brave in battle—good leaders."

These men were so very different from the Asherites we read about in the time of Israel's judges. They did not display mediocre or even "good" character; they were *excellent.* They were at the top, and no one could point a finger at them. They no longer shrank from their responsibilities, the very area they had failed in earlier. They became fearless. When it came to fighting, the men of Asher seemed to mature over the years.

We see the same qualities in the Bible's description of the forty thousand Asherites who went out in support of David. They are portrayed as "experienced soldiers prepared for battle" (1 Chronicles 12:36). And when King Hezekiah sent messengers to call the remnant of Israel to return to the Lord and celebrate the Passover, again the Asherites proved their worth. At a time when most of the people were ridiculing the king's messengers, the Asherites' response was different: "The couriers went from town to town in Ephraim and Manasseh, as far as Zebulun, but people scorned and ridiculed them. Nevertheless, some from Asher, Manasseh and Zebulun humbled themselves and went to Jerusalem" (2 Chronicles 30:10–11). The Asherites did not choose to follow the dissenters, but were willing to humble themselves. When most of the Israelites chose to turn away from God, these Asherites preferred to hold on to Him. Surely, any prosperity and provision they enjoyed was because of the fact that they knew who their God was and were confident in Him.

An Asherite in the New Testament

It is somewhat surprising that throughout the history of Israel, not one prominent person came forth from the tribe of Asher. We do not read of any judge, prophet or king arising from the men of Asher, although they were good leaders and excellent warriors. Yet it is also fascinating that the New Testament specifically records the name of a woman from this tribe and has good things to tell us about her:

> There was also a prophetess, Anna, the daughter of Phanuel, of the tribe of Asher. She was very old; she had lived with her husband seven years after her marriage, and then was a widow until she was eighty-four. She never left the temple but worshiped night and day, fasting and praying. Coming up to them at that very moment, she gave thanks to God and spoke about the child to all who were looking forward to the redemption of Jerusalem.
>
> Luke 2:36–38 NIV1984

Very little is said about Anna's personal life, other than that she was married for just seven years and then became a widow until she was eighty-four long years old. She must have suffered much emotional pain and social stigma. Can you imagine such a person being happy? But when we read about Anna, a picture of a happy person floods our minds. What was it that could have made her happy? The Bible makes clear the secrets of her happiness:

- She never left the Temple.
- She worshiped God night and day.
- She fasted and prayed.

What an incredible woman Anna from the tribe of Asher was. She knew her God and had built a strong relationship with Him, trusting in Him and lacking nothing. People around her may have made fun of her age and situation, but that did not bother her. She knew who her God was and found her strength in Him.

Anna was one of the few who waited with longing to see the Messiah. Surely she must have studied the Scriptures and lived every moment in the Temple, anticipating the fulfillment of God's promises. Instantly on seeing Joseph, Mary and the little baby in the Temple, Anna knew the Messiah had come. It was not just instinct that told her this; it must have been a revelation from the Holy Spirit. With great joy she thanked God, and she could not keep such news to herself. She spoke about it to everyone who awaited the coming of the Messiah, as she had. She was a true Asherite—a happy person richly fulfilled in the God whom she loved and worshiped.

Moses and the Tribe of Asher

When Moses blesses the tribe of Asher, he elaborates on Jacob's words over Asher and tells the Asherites that greater blessings are in store for them:

> Most blessed of sons is Asher; let him be favored by his brothers, and let him bathe his feet in oil. The bolts of your gates will be iron and bronze, and your strength will equal your days.
>
> Deuteronomy 33:24–25

The Message phrases it this way:

> Asher, best blessed of the sons! May he be the favorite of his brothers, his feet massaged in oil. Safe behind iron-clad doors and gates, your strength like iron as long as you live.

Moses declares that the Asherites will be the most blessed of all the sons of Jacob. In other words, they will be the happiest of them all. In addition, they will be the most liked by all their brothers. The other tribes will look up to the Asherites and respect them. The happiness of the Asherites will be contagious, and in turn, they will make all their brothers happy.

Moses then moves on to describe the extent of this tribe's prosperity. He affirms the words of Jacob over Asher—that the Asherites will indeed prosper. Their prosperity will be such that while others usually soak their feet in water after a long day, the Asherites will have the luxury of soaking their feet in oil, a privilege only those who were extremely rich could afford.

Moses adds that the Asherites will have no reason to fear anything or be anxious about their safety, for along with all their wealth, they will be protected behind doors locked with sturdy iron and bronze bolts. No one will be able to break in easily, so the Asherites will be secure.

Yet Moses does not stop even with that. He goes on to bless the Asherites with enough strength for each day. Moses seems to be telling the Asherites that no matter what enormous tasks await them, no matter how huge their challenges are, no matter how difficult life may get, they can rest assured because God will give them the strength they require for each day.

The people of Asher needed nothing more than this assurance. According to the words of both Jacob and Moses, they would be blessed, honored and prosperous. They would also be safe and have enough strength for every day of their lives. Certainly, the words of these blessings are enough reason to make the people of Asher happy!

Today's Application for Us

The knowledge of who God is not only brings joy, but also brings prosperity in many areas. People who trust God with their future find the joy of the Lord in every step of their way. The Asherites were not the only ones to experience this blessing. Let's learn from a few others. Isaac knew who his God was. He followed the footsteps of his father, Abraham, in worshiping Him. God appeared to Isaac and confirmed the promise He had made to Abraham to bless him, make his descendants as numerous as the stars in the sky and bless all the nations of the earth through him (see Genesis 26:3–4). God protected Isaac and his wife, Rebekah, while they were in Gerar. The Bible tells us that "Isaac planted crops in that land and the same year reaped a hundredfold, because the LORD blessed him" (Genesis 26:12).

The blessing of the Lord results in fruitfulness. Isaac continued to grow very wealthy. This made the Philistines envious. They had closed up all the wells his father Abraham's servants had dug, filling them with earth. Isaac reopened the wells and named them. Even though the Philistines argued over some of the wells and claimed ownership of them, Isaac did not worry over it. He simply left those wells for them and moved on, digging elsewhere. The Bible recounts that Isaac's servants dug several wells and found water in all of them (see Genesis 26:19–22). God provided water wherever Isaac dug.

God desires that we be fruitful. Jesus addressed His disciples, saying, "I am the vine; you are the branches. If you remain in me and I in you, you will bear much fruit; apart from me you can do nothing" (John 15:5). A life lived in Christ and with the knowledge of Christ will flourish and be prosperous. The apostle John wrote, "Beloved, I pray that you may prosper in all things and be in health, just as your soul prospers" (3 John 2 NKJV).

The disciples knew Jesus for three and a half years. They were an ordinary group of men who left everything they had—their families and their livelihood—and chose to follow Jesus. It was not easy to let go of everything and take the path unknown. But once Jesus came into their lives, everything changed. The disciples saw Jesus performing miracles, providing for their needs and protecting them. The gospel of Luke narrates how Jesus sent out the 72 to minister, and they "returned with joy and said, 'Lord, even the demons submit to us in your name'" (Luke 10:17).

The gospel of Mark says, "Then the disciples went out and preached everywhere, and the Lord worked with them and confirmed his word by the signs that accompanied it" (Mark 16:20). Before His death Jesus had promised, "Very truly I tell you, whoever believes in me will do the works I have been doing, and they will do even greater things than these, because I am going to the Father" (John 14:12).

A God-sent Gift

We were scheduled to dedicate our church building on December 18, 1994. The church members had given willingly and sacrificially toward the church's construction. We were in the last stages of completing the building, but we needed another Indian rupees 350,000 (just over $23,000 then). I had invited a well-known Indian evangelist whom I admired to be the special guest of honor. We had to take care of this man of God and host him, but we had no money in our hands.

At that time, our bank officials suggested that I take out a loan to cover the rest of the expenses, but my heart was not in it. Instead, I decided to get down on my knees and pray. I used to come to the church every morning and pray. Now we were nearing the "big day," and we still did not have the money we needed. Then one day while I was praying, the local AG chairman called and told me that there was a check waiting for me.

As happy as I was to hear that, I had never allowed the devil to steal my joy during the times I had spent praying. I had remained confident in God. People generally tend to confuse joy and happiness. Happiness depends on the happenings. When something good happens, we feel happy. But the difference with joy is that when we know God, we have joy despite our circumstances. All throughout that time I had remained joyful, trusting God to do a miracle. Once again, He did.

When I talked to the AG chairman about the check, I never asked him who had sent the money. My only question was, "How much did the person send?"

Startled, he answered, "It's a check for 385,000 rupees." He had expected that the first thing I would ask would be who had sent the money.

I explained to him, "It doesn't matter who sent the money. I know that my Jehovah Jireh has provided for us, and He sent the needed amount at the needed time. Truly, this money is God-sent!"

There was no other explanation. God had once again proved that He answers prayers and that He is faithful.

After hearing my reply, my AG chairman explained what had happened. A man in America had read about me and my ministry in a magazine. One night he kept tossing and turning on his bed, unable to sleep.

God spoke to him at that time and asked, *Why don't you send this amount of money to the person you read about?*

The next day, the man sent the amount that God had laid in his heart to our AG headquarters in Springfield, Missouri. The protocol to transfer a missions donation from America to India through this organization is rather involved, however, so the man had given the money a month prior to the day I had received it. But God in all His wisdom had arranged for us to have the money just at the right time. It made us all happy that God had provided for us. To this day, I do not know the identity of the person who gave that gift, but I am thankful that God had heard the cry of my heart.

Ways to Know Who God Is

During that final construction stage of our church, when it seemed as though we had reached a dead end, God proved that He is a living God and that He can provide a living answer at a dead end. Through that experience and many others, I have discovered the same thing that the Asherites learned from knowing who God is:

- God is the one who *protects* us.
- God is the one who *provides* for us.
- God is the one who *prospers* us.

I have also learned that there is a path we need to take if we want to know God at an intimate level so that our joy will be complete. This path consists of these steps:

Meditate on the attributes of God. The book of Psalms starts by talking about how a person can lead a blessed life: "Blessed is the one who does not walk in step with the wicked or stand in the way that sinners take or sit in the company of mockers, but whose delight is in the law of the LORD, and who meditates on his law day and night" (Psalm 1:1–2). The book of Exodus contains a beautiful revelation of the attributes of God: "The LORD, the LORD, the compassionate and gracious God, slow to anger, abounding in love and faithfulness, maintaining love to thousands, and forgiving wickedness, rebellion and sin" (Exodus 34:6–7). King David praised God in the midst of the people of Israel: "Yours, LORD, is the greatness and the power and the glory and the majesty and the splendor, for everything in heaven and earth is yours. Yours, LORD, is the kingdom; you are exalted as head over all" (1 Chronicles 29:11).

Maintain a godly life. As believers, we need to be careful about the wiles of the enemy, who constantly seeks to destroy us. We must not allow anything to distract us or cause us to deviate from the course God has planned for our lives. As the apostle Peter put it, "Dear friends, I urge you, as foreigners and exiles, to abstain from sinful desires, which wage war against your soul" (1 Peter 2:11). Writing to the church at Ephesus, the apostle Paul said, "As a prisoner for the Lord, then, I urge you to live a life worthy of the calling you have received" (Ephesians 4:1).

Manifest the presence of God in our lives. Our lives must reflect the God we worship. "No one has ever seen God; but if we love one another, God lives in us and his love is made complete in us" (1 John 4:12). God has promised us that He will abide with us if we abide in Him (see John 15:5–7). Even as we walk under the guidance of the Holy Spirit, we will remain hidden behind the glory of our Creator, and He will be magnified.

Master the abilities God has given us. The apostle Peter writes, "Each of you should use whatever gift you have received to serve others, as faithful stewards of God's grace in its various forms. If anyone speaks, they should do so . . . with the strength God provides, so that in all things God may be praised through Jesus Christ" (1 Peter 4:10–11). Each of us has a gift that God has given us. We must take time to identify it, master it and use it for the glory of God. Jesus taught that to him who was faithful with little, much would be given (see Luke 16:10). Writing to the church at Colossae, the apostle Paul said, "Whatever you do, work at it with all your heart, as working for the Lord, not for human masters, since you know that you will receive an inheritance from the Lord as a reward. It is the Lord Christ you are serving" (Colossians 3:23–24).

Model our lives after Christ. The apostle Paul strove to glorify God in everything. He was an evangelist and a church planter who did not allow anything to hinder his walk with the Lord. "Follow my example," he said, "as I follow the example of Christ" (1 Corinthians 11:1). The Bible also teaches us that, "Whoever claims to live in him must live as Jesus did" (1 John 2:6).

God wants His children to be like Him. In this life, there is nothing better than knowing Him. Asher and the Asherites show us that those who know who God is find themselves blessed by His provision and protection.

Our hearts' desire must be to know Him more. As children of God, let us meditate on His Word every day and live a life worthy of His calling. When people see us, they should not see us, but the God in us. Let's not let go of the life that God has given us, but let's serve Him to the best of our ability, even as we walk in His footsteps every day.

Let's Pray Together

Gracious and loving heavenly Father, thank You for Your providence, which we can clearly see all the way from the time of Asher and the Asherites to the present. You are concerned with even the smallest details of our lives. You protect us from dangers unseen, and You are compassionate and gracious, abundant in love and faithfulness.

We choose to praise You and submit our lives to Your calling. Thank You for Your gift of the Holy Spirit, who dwells in us. Reveal to each of us the specific gifts of the Holy Spirit that You have bestowed on us.

Our desire is to walk in Your ways and under Your blessings. We want to be a reflection of You for all to see.

In Jesus' name we pray, Amen.

10

Naphtali

Happy are those who speak good words,
for they will abound with the favor of God.

Prayer has always been an integral part of my life and ministry. During my pioneering days, as I walked and prayed in different parts of Bangalore I saw changes taking place—people being saved and added to the church. As I saw the fruit that was produced, God placed in my heart a desire to travel to different places and pray for situations to change, blessing these places in the name of Jesus. Accordingly, in the early 1990s we started our "Prayer Penetration" ministry, in which a team of pastors and believers would travel to different cities and states to pray. With our God-given burden, we would pray for the Kingdom of God to be established in those areas.

In the year 2002, one hundred of us walked from Bangalore to Mysore to pronounce the blessings of God over the cities and towns we passed. There is a total of 128 kilometers between the two cities, so we divided our people into groups to cover the distance. Each group walked and prayed for a distance of 10 kilometers and then was picked up by a bus and dropped in Mysore, our destination. We passed many towns where the Gospel was not welcome and where building churches was not allowed. These were hard places that needed Christ. We bound every sort of demonic oppression in these places and declared the power, glory and blessings of God over them.

God enabled me to walk 53 kilometers on that day. We finally reached Mysore and went to a particular area where the pastor had been trying to get a permit to build a church for many years. We prayed with faith and claimed the victory in Jesus' name. In just ten days' time, permission was granted to build that church. Later, we traveled to Mysore again for the ground-breaking at the church site and rejoiced together over the miracle God had done.

Today as we see the towns we passed by and prayed for, we see that God's mighty hand has been at work. Many, many churches have been built, including several that God opened the doors for us to build. We had gone in person to these places and prayed without sitting in the comfort of our church, and now we can see the changes our words of blessing effected. Our words have power.

Blessings follow good words. First Samuel 25 tells us the story of Abigail, Nabal's wife. Nabal was a wealthy man who owned a great number of goats and sheep. David and his band of men, who were in the wilderness of Paran at that time, were very good to Nabal's shepherds; their presence gave the shepherds a sense of security. As sheep-shearing time came, David sent men to Nabal to request that he send David's band some food. Nabal arrogantly refused and humiliated them. This angered David, who prepared to attack him.

News of the coming attack reached Abigail through a servant. Acting promptly, she packed a large quantity of food and loaded it on some donkeys. She took the food to David, fell at his feet and begged his forgiveness for her husband's wickedness. She attempted to conciliate David with her gift, and she pleaded with him not to kill her husband. She said that God Himself would fight on David's behalf and avenge him. Abigail's wise words made David change his mind, and he abandoned his plan for revenge. Spoken at the right time, her prudent words averted unnecessary bloodshed.

Those who speak good words will abound with the favor of God. In Genesis 49 Jacob blesses his son Naphtali, and one of the translations of his blessing says that Naphtali will speak beautiful words. Moses' prophecy over the tribe of Naphtali in Deuteronomy 33 says they will be a people blessed and favored by the Lord. Here are a few more verses from the Bible that emphasize the power of the spoken word:

> Do not let any unwholesome talk come out of your mouths, but only what is helpful for building others up according to their needs, that it may benefit those who listen.
>
> Ephesians 4:29

> From the fruit of their lips people enjoy good things, but the unfaithful have an appetite for violence.
>
> Proverbs 13:2

> The tongue has the power of life and death, and those who love it will eat its fruit.
>
> Proverbs 18:21

> Let your conversation be always full of grace, seasoned with salt, so that you may know how to answer everyone.
>
> Colossians 4:6

> Whoever would love life and see good days must keep their tongue from evil and their lips from deceitful speech.
>
> 1 Peter 3:10

As we begin to comprehend that there is great power in the words we speak, let's make a conscious effort to speak beautiful words, words that will change the unpleasant situations around us, words of healing, power and blessing.

The Birth of Naphtali

The scuffle between the two sisters, Leah and Rachel, kept building with the birth of more sons. What started with Leah just wanting the love and affection of her husband slowly developed into a fierce fight between the sisters. Each wanted to show the other that she was better, and their relationship only grew worse over time as a result.

Rachel had given her maidservant, Bilhah, to Jacob, and Bilhah in turn had given birth to Dan. Rachel exulted, for she felt that God had finally stood up for her and had vindicated her. To Rachel's delight, Bilhah conceived again and gave birth to another son. "Then Rachel said, 'I have had a great struggle with my sister, and I have won.' So she named him Naphtali" (Genesis 30:8).

Imagine how Rachel must have felt as she held a second son, Naphtali, in her arms, even though she herself was unable to bear children. She felt a twinge of victory over Leah. No wonder she gave vent to those feelings when she declared that she had won her struggle against her sister. After all those years of enviously watching Leah with her children, Rachel did not have to bother anymore, for she finally had two sons through her maidservant that she could call her own. The birth of Naphtali filled Rachel with a sense of victory over Leah.

Naphtali is another of the "silent" sons of Jacob. After his birth, nothing else noteworthy is mentioned of him in the rest of Genesis, other than that he is named with Jacob's sons in the list of those who accompanied their father to Egypt (see Genesis 46:24).

Jacob's Prophetic Words over Naphtali

If the words of Jacob to his son Asher had left Asher startled and marveling, then his words to Naphtali must have left Naphtali absolutely dumbfounded:

> Naphtali is a doe set free that bears beautiful fawns.

> Genesis 49:21

Or as *The Message* puts it,

Naphtali is a deer running free that gives birth to lovely fawns.

On seeing Naphtali at his side, Jacob compared him to a doe, a female deer. Naphtali would not be as aggressive as a lion, like his brother Judah. He would not be as lazy as a donkey lying between the saddlebags, like his brother Issachar. Nor would he be as crafty as a viper, like his brother Dan. Rather, Naphtali would be a quick-footed doe who, after a time of captivity, is set free and begins to enjoy its freedom.

The phrase about bearing beautiful fawns has more than one possible meaning behind it. The footnote in my Bible clarifies that Jacob's words could also be translated as "he utters beautiful words." If that were the translation, perhaps Jacob had noticed that as the boy Naphtali grew up, comparatively he was more on the soft side than his brothers. Maybe Naphtali displayed a gentle personality and a quiet spirit, but when he opened his mouth to speak, he amazed those around him.

Whatever the circumstances, all does not seem lost for Naphtali, the last of the maidservants' sons to receive his blessing from Jacob. Later on, the prophet Isaiah asserts that a glorious future awaits those from the tribe of Naphtali, along with those from Zebulun. One day the Messiah Himself would arise in their land and spend much of His time ministering among them (see Isaiah 9:1–2; Matthew 4:12–16). Light would dawn on a dark land, and as a doe set free would enjoy its freedom, the people would rejoice as their gloom turned into joy.

The Naphtalites in the Old Testament

Let's turn our attention to Naphtali's descendants. Many of the Naphtalites seemed happy simply to follow the crowd, not wanting to push themselves to achieve something. Like some of the other tribes, the men of Naphtali failed to drive out the Canaanites from the portion of land they inherited. They continued living among the Canaanites, which went directly against God's instruction. Also like the other tribes, in certain places the Naphtalites subjected the people of Canaan to forced labor (see Judges 1:33).

From such a tribe, however, arose Barak, a man who stood with and helped Deborah against Jabin, king of Canaan, and Sisera, his commander. This was during the time when Deborah led Israel as its judge. When the Canaanites' oppression of Israel became unbearable, the people called to the Lord for help. Deborah called for Barak, who was from the tribe of Naphtali, and instructed him that the Lord was commanding him to take ten thousand men of Naphtali and Zebulun and fight, for the Lord would deliver Sisera into his hands (see Judges 4).

What a God-given opportunity, with God Himself promising to deliver Sisera and his troops into Barak's hands. Did the Naphtalite Barak seize the opportunity? Not by himself. Instead, he beseeched Deborah to come with him and refused to go without her (see Judges 4:8). Deborah then made it clear to Barak that while God was offering him the honor of conquering Sisera, he was going to lose that honor to a woman. Barak did not mind that. While he was willing to do everything in his power to help Deborah fight the battle, it seems to me that he did not want to be in the limelight.

The men of Naphtali responded to Barak's call, along with those from Zebulun. Together they fought the Canaanites, which won them Deborah's appreciation. In her victory song, she says of Naphtali and Zebulun together, "The people of Zebulun risked their very lives; so did Naphtali on the terraced fields" (Judges 5:18). These courageous warriors fought valiantly in the thick of battle. They could be relied upon.

Likewise, when Gideon called for men from the tribes of Manasseh, Asher, Zebulun and Naphtali to come to his aid in the fight against the Midianites, the men of Naphtali were quick to respond and pursue the enemy (see Judges 7:23). The Naphtalites also supported David and defected to him in great numbers. These were men of great caliber. Among those who joined David, 1,000 were officers and 37,000 were trained warriors (see 1 Chronicles 12:34). When David eventually was crowned king, men from Naphtali, along with those from Issachar and Zebulun, brought food and supplies for a celebration that lasted three days (see 1 Chronicles 12:40).

One man whose name stands out in the Old Testament and who contributed much from the tribe of Naphtali was Huram, whom King Solomon himself relied on:

> King Solomon sent to Tyre and brought Huram, whose mother was a widow from the tribe of Naphtali and whose father was from Tyre and a skilled craftsman in bronze. Huram was filled with wisdom, with understanding and with knowledge to do all kinds of bronze work. He came to King Solomon and did all the work assigned to him.
>
> 1 Kings 7:13–14

Like his father, Huram was greatly skilled and widely experienced. King Solomon had him help in the building of the Temple. First Kings 7 describes the detailed work that King Solomon assigned to Huram, which this craftsman painstakingly and faithfully completed. Again a man from Naphtali was doing distinguished work, but I think that like Barak, he probably did not desire to draw any attention to himself.

Unfortunately, at some point the Naphtalites opened their doors to the worship of the neighboring heathen gods and goddesses. We read that during the reign of King Josiah, who vehemently opposed idol worship, the king had to take serious steps to purge the practice among them: "In the towns of Manasseh, Ephraim and Simeon, as far as Naphtali, and in the ruins around them, he tore down the altars and the Asherah poles and crushed the idols to powder and cut to pieces all the incense altars throughout Israel" (2 Chronicles 34:6–7). Even as far as the land of Naphtali, the people were involved in such intense idol worship that Josiah had to purge the entire place. Ultimately, the Assyrians attacked the people of Israel and took captive the tribe of Naphtali.

Tiglath-Pileser, king of Assyria, "took Gilead and Galilee, including all the land of Naphtali, and deported the people to Assyria" (2 Kings 15:29).

Moses and the Tribe of Naphtali

While Jacob simply seemed to appreciate Naphtali in his prophecy over him, Moses builds on Jacob's words and blesses Naphtali abundantly. He says about the tribe of Naphtali,

> Naphtali is abounding with the favor of the LORD and is full of his blessing; he will inherit southward to the lake.
>
> Deuteronomy 33:23

The Message says,

> Naphtali brims with blessings, spills over with GOD's blessings as he takes possession of the sea and southland.

Just as Moses described, the tribe of Naphtali inherited the land to the south (see Joshua 19:32–39). Further, all Moses could see was the favor of God resting bountifully on Naphtali. The picture he gives is that of a vessel not only full, but spilling over. Naphtali's blessings would not only be for the people of Naphtali, but would flow over to others.

How true were Moses' words, for with the coming of the Messiah from the land of Naphtali, not only were the people of Naphtali blessed, but their blessing overflowed to the rest of the world.

Today's Application for Us

Words of blessing are so powerful, and good words bring such favor. Besides learning this from Naphtali and his tribe, we can see it elsewhere in Scripture. Think about the story of Balaam. The children of Israel were God's chosen people, among whom

He performed many signs and wonders. He brought them out of the land of Egypt, where they had been oppressed under slavery, and He led them into the Promised Land. He was with them all along the way, guarding them and guiding them.

During their journey, the children of Israel met with a lot of opposition, but God gave them victory. He struck fear in the heart of all the neighboring nations when they realized that He was fighting for the Israelites. The people of Moab were terrified because the Israelites camped in the plains of Moab were large in number (see Numbers 22:1–3). So Balak, king of Moab, summoned Balaam and said,

> A people has come out of Egypt; they cover the face of the land and have settled next to me. Now come and put a curse on these people, because they are too powerful for me. Perhaps then I will be able to defeat them and drive them out of the land. For I know that whoever you bless is blessed, and whoever you curse is cursed.
>
> Numbers 22:5–6

Notice the power King Balak attributed to words—positive or negative. Balaam inquired of the Lord, who told him that he was not to comply with the request of the king of Moab, because God Himself had chosen to bless the children of Israel.

On hearing Balaam's refusal, King Balak felt that maybe he had not sent the right people to speak to Balaam the first time. He next tried sending distinguished officials who were more in number to summon Balaam with the promise that he would receive great rewards for cursing the children of Israel. Balaam still refused to go. He knew that the children of Israel had the favor of God, so his efforts to curse them would be of no use. He refused the second time, expressing that regardless of the nature of the reward, he could not go against the command of the Lord.

Later that night, however, "God came to Balaam and said, 'Since these men have come to summon you, go with them, but do only what I tell you'" (Numbers 22:20).

Having received a command from the Lord, Balaam expressed to King Balak that he would only speak that which the Lord commanded him. Balaam then met with the Lord, received a word from Him and proceeded to speak it over Israel. The words that he spoke were words of blessing and not a curse.

The Moabite king was furious, but he decided to try taking Balaam to another spot from where he could see Israel and curse them. After inquiring from the Lord and receiving another word from Him, Balaam proceeded to pronounce not a curse, but another blessing over Israel.

By this time, the king was at his wits' end. He told Balaam in frustration, "Neither curse them at all nor bless them at all!" (Numbers 23:25). The third attempt of the king to pronounce a curse over Israel through Balaam failed miserably. Filled with the Spirit of God, Balaam pronounced blessing after blessing. God used the same man who had been called to curse the children of Israel to pronounce seven blessings over them. When God's favor rests on a person, the attempts of any man to speak a curse over that person will only fail.

Jesus said, "But the things that come out of a person's mouth come from the heart, and these defile them" (Matthew 15:18). In other words, it is that which is deep inside our hearts that takes the form of words and proceeds from our mouths. We must be careful about the words we speak, for the Word of God teaches us that we are accountable for every idle word: "But I tell you that everyone will have to give account on the day of judgment for every empty word they have spoken. For by your words you will be acquitted, and by your words you will be condemned" (Matthew 12:36–37).

In the New Testament we read about Stephen, who was full of God's grace, power and wisdom. God used him to perform great signs and wonders among the people (see Acts 6:8). But Stephen faced opposition from those who were unable to accept his preaching and teaching. His opposers failed to win arguments with him, for they could not counter his wisdom, so instead they raised false reports and testimonies against him.

When questioned before the Sanhedrin, Stephen was not afraid. He spoke out with boldness and courage, "Was there ever a prophet your ancestors did not persecute? They even killed those who predicted the coming of the Righteous One. And now you have betrayed and murdered him" (Acts 7:52). The words that came out of Stephen's mouth shot like arrows and further angered the members of the Sanhedrin. Even with death sneering at him, however, Stephen remained unafraid. Ultimately, his enemies dragged him out of the city and stoned him to death. Stephen did not curse his persecutors, but rather, he chose to speak words of forgiveness over their lives: "While they were stoning him, Stephen prayed, 'Lord Jesus, receive my spirit.' Then he fell on his knees and cried out, 'Lord, do not hold this sin against them.' When he had said this, he fell asleep" (verses 59–60). Stephen knew that good words bring God's favor.

Pronouncing God's Blessings

Thinking of the blessings good words bring reminds me of some other events of the year 2002. Christianity caught aflame and continued to grow in India. Revival was spreading across the nation, and the number of churches began to increase. At that time, the opposition also began to increase. The chief minister of a neighboring state passed an anti-conversion bill that contained a provision aimed at stopping people from becoming Christians. During that time, the Lord gave me a burden to pray for those in that state who were going through this persecution. He also told me to take a bus and travel throughout that neighboring state to pray.

I did as the Lord had instructed me. Over a period of 5 days, 50 of us traveled by bus to 45 locations, a trip that covered over 4,500 kilometers. We went to more than 35 districts in that state, gathered the pastors and leaders of the churches in those places and challenged them to declare victory and pronounce the blessings of God over their state, districts and cities. We encouraged the believers there to remain fearless even in the face of adversity, because we are God's chosen children and He will never leave us nor forsake us. The government was very strict about the new law and was doing everything it could to oppress us. As a team we kept moving from one place to another, regardless of sickness and fatigue.

I have always admired the boldness and courage of the apostle Paul. He never gave up, regardless of the opposition he faced. Inspired by his life and by the Word of God, I decided to go near the chief minister's house and pray. It was a bold step. Though I was unsure how I could get near the house physically, in my spirit I was like a charging lion. I went as close as possible, sat in my car and kept praying for 44 minutes. More than 50 officers holding their weapons were stationed in front of that house, but not one of them came to my car to ask what I was doing there. Within a few months the anti-conversion bill was canceled. All glory to God!

We can declare the promises of God over imposing situations, and true to His Word, God will turn them around for our good.

Ways to Speak Life and Blessings

God has breathed life into us and has given us the ability to speak life into dead situations. We are His children, and we have His favor. We should always be conscious of that, realizing He can do the impossible and trusting Him always. God is able to do much more than what we can think or imagine. My experiences have helped me realize the following ways through which we can walk into victory:

Think differently. Our thoughts need not be conformed to the pattern of this world. The Word of God teaches us that God can turn an impossible situation around. We need to bear that in mind. Joshua and Caleb were sent with ten other men to spy out the land of Canaan. While ten men saw only the size of the giants in the land and considered taking it an impossible task, Joshua and

Caleb thought differently (see Numbers 13:30). As a result, they were the only two out of the twelve spies who had the privilege of entering the Promised Land. At another time, we see the people of Israel terrified because of another giant. While grown men were afraid to face Goliath in battle, a young lad named David stepped up to face the challenge. His thoughts were different. He told King Saul, "The LORD who rescued me from the paw of the lion and the paw of the bear will rescue me from the hand of this Philistine" (1 Samuel 17:37). David went on to conquer the giant. Never think a situation is impossible. We need to think as Jesus told us—that nothing is impossible with God.

Trust God to intervene. God is able to intervene and do a miracle. He has never let down those who trust in Him. "So do not fear, for I am with you; do not be dismayed, for I am your God. I will strengthen you and help you; I will uphold you with my righteous right hand" (Isaiah 41:10). Through the prophet Isaiah, God also spoke this: "When you pass through the waters, I will be with you; and when you pass through the rivers, they will not sweep over you. When you walk through the fire, you will not be burned; the flames will not set you ablaze" (Isaiah 43:2).

Talk in faith and declare victory over the situation. As the Bible says, there is power in our words. God spoke everything into existence. Jesus said, "Therefore I tell you, whatever you ask for in prayer, believe that you have received it, and it will be yours" (Mark 11:24). When we confess in faith, we truly will see God's rewards.

Transform the situation through the power of the Holy Spirit. We can do nothing without the help of the Holy Spirit. We must depend on Him to take charge of any situation and work things out for us. Jesus told His disciples, "When you are brought before synagogues, rulers and authorities, do not worry about how you will defend yourselves or what you will say, for the Holy Spirit will teach you at that time what you should say" (Luke 12:11–12).

Testify to the goodness and favor of God. The psalmist said of what God can do, "My mouth will tell of your righteous deeds, of your saving acts all day long—though I know not how to relate them all" (Psalm 71:15). People around us should not only see God in us, but should also hear His goodness and favor being confessed from our lips. The psalmist also said, "I will speak of your statutes before kings and will not be put to shame" (Psalm 119:46). Our words should be words of faith that declare victory over adverse situations because God is able to transform them.

As we saw from looking at Naphtali, his tribe and others in Scripture, when good words are spoken the favor of God abounds. May our lives always testify to God's goodness.

Let's Pray Together

Gracious and loving heavenly Father, thank You for setting us free from captivity and filling us with unending joy. Transform our minds so that we can see things from Your perspective. With You, nothing is impossible.

We place our trust in You and You alone. We will wait on You to intervene, not moving in our own might, but in Yours. We will speak aloud Your Word and truth, using the sword of the Spirit to battle in spiritual realms.

We will use our words to build up and not break down. We will control our tongues and speak blessings over others. Like the words spoken over Naphtali and the Naphtalites, let our good words bring Your favor and blessings. Let our lives be a testament of Your love and goodness for all to see.

In Jesus' name we pray, Amen.

11

Joseph

Happy are those who recognize
the hand of God in their lives,
for they will be blessed beyond measure.

My life in the service of the Lord has been a series of miracles, one after the other, testifying of His undeniable goodness and total control over my life and ministry. When we were holding our church services in a rented building, God placed a dream in my heart for a church building of our own. I spent many days in prayer, seeking God concerning this. One day I received a phone call from a person who said he wanted to meet me. When I went to see him, he told me that he wanted to gift me land for the church building. I was so excited that I told the news to my family, the church and the organization I belonged to—everyone! We all were overjoyed at the miracle God had done.

It took us nearly two months to complete all the necessary paperwork. Once everything was ready, we fixed a day for the signing of the agreement and the official transfer of the land in the name of the Assemblies of God. The key leaders of the organization came to Bangalore for the signing.

The evening before the appointed day, I got a call from the donor of the land. He wanted to meet with me. When I went to see him, he calmly told me that he had changed his mind about giving the land to us. Certain people who were jealous of us had poisoned his mind against us, and he told me he no longer wanted to donate the property.

I was so shocked! I did not know what to say, so I just stood up, looked at him and said, "You keep the land; I will keep the vision."

I did not plead, I did not beg, I just said those words and left the place. I was furious. I started my car, made a sharp turn and rapidly drove away. I was so devastated that I went to an ice cream parlor nearby and ate sixteen scoops of ice cream!

After a while, I went home. I did not tell anyone about what had happened. With the excuse that I was not feeling well, I skipped my dinner. After everyone had gone to bed, I went out to pray. I walked on the deserted street near our house that night and cried out to God.

What do I do now, Lord? I cried. That was the question that my perplexed mind kept repeating. At exactly 1:45 a.m., God told me to go to bed. With peace in my heart that God was in control, I calmly obeyed.

The next morning I got ready, and as per the original plan, I went to pick up the person who earlier had said he would give us the land. I stopped my car at his doorstep and honked. He came out with some files in his hand, and without saying a word he got into my car. It was a long drive to the meeting place where the organization leaders were waiting, and we passed it in complete silence, with only a CD playing in the background. I had no idea what was going on in his mind. I simply let God take control.

Once we reached the place, I greeted everyone with a smile. I told them I did not have much to say and asked the man whom I had brought to go ahead with whatever he had to say. What he said stunned me!

"At exactly 1:45 a.m. early this morning," he announced, "God told me to give the land to His son because He has a great ministry through his life!"

That was exactly the same time that God had filled my heart with peace and told me to go to bed. We all signed the papers and it was official; the land belonged to the Assemblies of God now. God had done an amazing miracle yet again.

This incident had a huge impact in my life. I learned that people may make promises and in the course of time change their minds, but it is always best to trust in God. I determined to move through life with my focus only on the vision God has given me and not on people, because people change, but God never changes.

Recognizing the hand of God in our lives brings blessings. Abraham's story in the book of Genesis reveals his unwavering confidence in the God who had called him. Abraham was a man rich in sheep, goats, cattle and servants, but he had no children of his own. God promised to give Abraham a son and told him his descendants would be as innumerable as the stars in the sky (see Genesis 15:5). Abraham was an old man when God spoke that promise to him. Sarah, his wife, was past child-bearing age as well. Besides that, many years then passed with no change after the promise, but Abraham held on to God. Though circumstances said there was no chance of this couple giving birth to a child, Abraham knew that God was able to do in their lives what He had spoken (see Romans 4:18–21). At a hundred years of age, Abraham's faith was honored and God blessed him with his son Isaac.

In Genesis 49, Jacob blessed the son he cherished the most, Joseph, with strength, abundance and the choicest blessings of heaven. It is easy to recognize the hand of God in Joseph's life. In Deuteronomy 33, Moses' prophecy over the tribes of Joseph's sons—Ephraim and Manasseh—is a reiteration of Jacob's prophecy. Moses speaks God's strength, abundance, favor, majesty and choicest blessings over them. Here are a few verses from the Bible that speak of the great plans God has for His children who hold on to Him in every circumstance:

And we know that in all things God works for the good of those who love him, who have been called according to his purpose.

Romans 8:28

"What no eye has seen, what no ear has heard, and what no human mind has conceived"—the things God has prepared for those who love him . . .

1 Corinthians 2:9

I know that you can do all things; no purpose of yours can be thwarted.

Job 42:2

. . . being confident of this, that he who began a good work in you will carry it on to completion until the day of Christ Jesus.

Philippians 1:6

"Today I have made you a fortified city, an iron pillar and a bronze wall to stand against the whole land—against the kings of Judah, its officials, its priests and the people of the land. They will fight against you but will not overcome you, for I am with you and will rescue you," declares the LORD.

Jeremiah 1:18–19

As we read about how Joseph stayed true to God in the midst of many trying situations and see how God lifted him up and blessed him richly, let it motivate us to stand strong in our faith in the God who has promised to be with us till the end of our days.

The Birth of Joseph

Leah continued giving birth to children and was even blessed with the birth of a daughter, Dinah (see Genesis 30:21). In the meantime, it appears that Rachel was content with the two sons her maidservant had given birth to, Dan and Naphtali. We hear of no more disputes, no more arguments between the sisters. Leah must have been busy taking care of her eight sons and one daughter, while Rachel seemed satisfied with the two sons at her feet.

The very Rachel whom we had earlier seen fighting with her husband about giving her children and fighting with her sister about giving her mandrakes seems to have settled down. At that point, God decided to work: "Then God remembered Rachel; he listened to her and opened her womb" (Genesis 30:22 NIV1984). Notice three things that God did for Rachel:

- He remembered.
- He listened.
- He opened.

God never forgot Rachel. Just as He had done for Leah, He heard Rachel's every cry and did what she least expected, when she least expected it—He opened her womb. "She became pregnant and gave birth to a son and said, 'God has taken away my disgrace.' She named him Joseph, and said, 'May the LORD add to me another son'" (Genesis 30:23–24 NIV1984).

What joy Rachel must have experienced when at last she found herself pregnant with a child of her own. God had blessed her as well. She no longer would have a reason to put her head down in shame. Anticipating more blessings from God, she quickly voiced her desire that He would bless her with another son after she delivered Joseph. Her first son's birth convinced her that God had removed her disgrace at last.

Genesis has much to say about Joseph, much more than it records about any of the other sons of Jacob. More than ten chapters of that Bible book are devoted to Joseph's story. Let's look at the hand of God in some of the events of Joseph's life.

Joseph and His Brothers

A look at Joseph's life makes it obvious why Jacob chose to love this son more than any of his other sons. Joseph was born to

Jacob's favorite wife, Rachel, when Jacob was well advanced in age. Jacob loved the pair of them so much that when he went to meet his brother, Esau, he took precautions to ensure that no harm would befall Rachel and Joseph. He set them at the very end of his family group, far behind the maidservants and their children or Leah and her children (see Genesis 33:1–2).

Jacob lavished his love on Joseph and made him a special "richly ornamented robe" (Genesis 37:3 NIV1984). Their father's partiality angered the rest of the brothers, who began to hate Joseph so much that they "could not speak a kind word to him" (verse 4). To make things worse, Joseph had a dream in which he saw all his brothers bowing to him. Unable to contain himself, he shared his dream with them. How much more his brothers hated him for that!

As if that were not enough, Joseph had yet another dream in which he saw his father and mother, along with his brothers, bowing down to him. He disclosed everything to his family, infuriating his brothers even more and making them extremely jealous. Not only did he carry tales about them to their father; he also received the best and most expensive gifts from Jacob (see Genesis 37:2). And he had such ridiculous and unimaginable dreams. How they must have gossiped about him, made fun of him and even imagined life without him. Hence, when the opportunity came to do something about the situation, they did not think twice.

In previous chapters, we talked about the role of some of the other brothers in the events that followed, but let's look at things this time from Joseph's point of view. Jacob had sent Joseph to check on his brothers, who had taken the flocks out to graze, and bring back word. The brothers were not where their father thought they would be, so Joseph had to go in search of them (see Genesis 37:12–18). Perhaps the brothers were not happy to see Joseph approaching—besides the wild dreams he had, Joseph had previously given their father a bad report about them. When they recognized him, they plotted to kill "that dreamer," as they called him, and then see just how his dreams could come true.

Joseph unsuspectingly walked right into their hands. Thankfully, he had at least a couple of brothers who were unwilling to commit such a murder. Reuben did not like the idea of killing Joseph and suggested that they throw him into a cistern instead (so he could later return and rescue the boy). Taking away Joseph's ornate robe, the brothers threw him into the pit. Later, they saw Ishmaelite merchants coming their way, and this time Judah bargained with his brothers to sell Joseph instead of killing their own flesh and blood. They agreed to the idea and sold Joseph for twenty shekels of silver.

After this betrayal, the brothers then took Joseph's special robe and stained it with the blood of a goat they had killed. They took the robe back to their father and lied to him, saying that they had found the robe and that it appeared to belong to Joseph (see Genesis 37:19–36). Jacob concluded that a wild animal had killed the son whom he loved the most, and he mourned uncontrollably for the boy.

Little did the brothers realize that what they had done was more than a result of their uncontrolled emotions. It was the supernatural hand of God at work, fulfilling His greater purposes for them and for all mankind. Joseph himself, however, would realize this and tell it to his brothers much later, after he revealed his identity to them in Egypt. He could recognize the hand of God in his life, and he was indeed blessed beyond measure because of it.

Joseph in Egypt

It did not take Joseph long to realize that what his brothers had done against him to destroy him, God would take and turn for the good. As he stayed faithful, he began to see God's favor on his life everywhere he went. In Egypt the Ishmaelite merchants sold Joseph to Potiphar, "one of Pharaoh's officials, the captain of the guard" (Genesis 37:36; 39:1). Yet the hand of God was so real upon Joseph's life that even in slavery he prospered:

The LORD was with Joseph so that he prospered, and he lived in the house of his Egyptian master. When his master saw that the LORD was with him and that the LORD gave him success in everything he did, Joseph found favor in his eyes and became his attendant. Potiphar put him in charge of his household, and he entrusted to his care everything he owned.

Genesis 39:2–4

Something in Joseph's life stood out and caused Potiphar to observe that there was a supernatural hand behind Joseph's success. He soon made Joseph his attendant and made him responsible for absolutely everything in his household. God honored Potiphar and blessed him "because of Joseph" (verse 5). Potiphar trusted Joseph completely and saw no reason to worry about anything with Joseph in charge.

Things did not remain as pleasant as they seemed for Joseph, however. Potiphar's wife tried to entice him into a relationship, but conscious of his obligation to his master and his fear of God, Joseph adamantly refused to have anything to do with her (see Genesis 39:6–10). Finding him strong in his convictions, she was unable to get hold of him, so she falsely accused him of taking advantage of her (see verses 11–18). Infuriated, Potiphar had Joseph put in prison for no real fault of his own.

Again Joseph found himself in a terrible situation, thrown into an Egyptian prison with no hope of release. Maybe he wondered how such a thing could have happened to him after he had been faithful and true to God in spite of his circumstances. Yet even in that bleak situation God was with Joseph, working it all out for his good. God continued to give him success in all he did. Amazingly, even in the prison "the LORD was with him; he showed him kindness and granted him favor in the eyes of the prison warden" (verse 21).

One day Joseph happened to see Pharaoh's chief cupbearer and chief baker, who were also in custody, looking downcast. While he could have ignored them and walked away, Joseph inquired as to why they looked sad. Both of them said that some dreams were troubling them because they did not understand them. Trusting God, Joseph gave both of them the interpretation of their dreams. His interpretations proved correct; in time the baker was put to death, while the cupbearer was released.

Joseph requested that the cupbearer remember him to Pharaoh, which the cupbearer unfaithfully forgot to do (see Genesis 40). Yet two years later, Pharaoh himself had two dreams that all the magicians and wise men of Egypt could not interpret for him. Finally, the cupbearer remembered Joseph and mentioned him to Pharaoh, who immediately had Joseph brought to the palace. With the wisdom that God gave him, Joseph interpreted Pharaoh's dreams. He told Pharaoh that God had revealed there would be seven years of abundance in Egypt, followed by seven years of famine.

Listening to the extensive plan Joseph suggested for dealing with the famine, Pharaoh decided that the best person to carry out the plan effectively—the person in whom dwelt the Spirit of God—was Joseph himself (see Genesis 41:1–38). Pharaoh told Joseph, "Since God has made all this known to you, there is no one so discerning and wise as you. You shall be in charge of my palace, and all my people are to submit to your orders. Only with respect to the throne will I be greater than you" (verses 39–40). Joseph was only thirty years old at that time, but he excelled in his planning because of the wisdom that came to him from God (see verses 46–57).

During the famine, Joseph's father, Jacob, soon learned that there was no shortage of grain in Egypt. We looked in earlier chapters at the story of how Jacob sent ten of his sons to Egypt to buy grain, keeping back only Benjamin, whom he did not want to risk losing. On seeing his brothers, Joseph recognized them, although they did not recognize him. To test their integrity and determine whether they had changed, he accused them of being spies. To prove that they were not, they shared their family background with him. In passing, they mentioned their elderly father and a younger brother who was still at home. At that point Joseph detained Simeon and ordered the rest to return home and bring their youngest brother, Benjamin, back with them.

You can imagine Jacob's reaction to the thought of losing the second of Rachel's two sons. To no avail the brothers tried to convince him to send Benjamin back with them, but he refused. Eventually, however, the family had nothing to eat, so Judah stood guarantee for Benjamin and persuaded Jacob to send him with them to Egypt.

Confident that his brothers had changed, Joseph finally revealed his true identity to them through a series of dramatic events. Here was the brother whom they supposed had died a slave in Egypt— very much alive. In fact, he was alive and well and second only to Pharaoh in that prosperous land.

After all they had done to harm him, Joseph could have been harsh toward his brothers. Instead, he forgave them and recognized the hand of God in everything that had transpired. "God sent me ahead of you to preserve for you a remnant on earth and to save your lives by a great deliverance," he told them. "So then, it was not you who sent me here, but God" (Genesis 45:7–8).

After revealing himself to his father, who rejoiced that his son was alive, as a true son Joseph provided a place for his family to settle in the land of Goshen and took care of them. He also made his brothers promise that the Israelites would one day take his remains with them to the Promised Land (see Genesis 50:24–25; Exodus 13:19). Little did Joseph's brothers know that all the events that had taken place were part of God's great plan to protect them from destruction during the famine, in order to fulfill His greater purposes for the world. What made Joseph blessed, however, was that he recognized the hand of God in his life.

Jacob's Prophetic Words over Joseph

Having spoken prophetic words of blessing over ten of his sons, sons whom he had fathered through Leah and the maidservants

Zilpah and Bilhah, Jacob then turned his attention to the two sons of Rachel. He looked first at Joseph, his dear son born of his dearest wife. God had chosen to restore this son, whom Jacob had long thought was dead. Jacob had much to declare over Joseph, whom he referred to as the prince among his brothers:

> Joseph is a fruitful vine, a fruitful vine near a spring, whose branches climb over a wall. With bitterness archers attacked him; they shot at him with hostility, but his bow remained steady, his strong arms stayed limber, because of the hand of the Mighty One of Jacob, because of the Shepherd, the Rock of Israel, because of your father's God, who helps you, because of the Almighty, who blesses you with blessings of the skies above, blessings of the deep springs below, blessings of the breast and womb. Your father's blessings are greater than the blessings of the ancient mountains, than the bounty of the age-old hills. Let all these rest on the head of Joseph, on the brow of the prince among his brothers.

> Genesis 49:22–26

The Message interestingly says it this way:

> Joseph is a wild donkey, a wild donkey by a spring, spirited donkeys on a hill. The archers with malice attacked, shooting their hate-tipped arrows; but he held steady under fire, his bow firm, his arms limber, with the backing of the Champion of Jacob, the Shepherd, the Rock of Israel. The God of your father—may he help you! And may The Strong God—may he give you his blessings, blessings tumbling out of the skies, blessings bursting up from the Earth—blessings of breasts and womb. May the blessings of your father exceed the blessings of the ancient mountains, surpass the delights of the eternal hills; may they rest on the head of Joseph, on the brow of the one consecrated among his brothers.

Without stopping to take a breath, Jacob spoke word after word over Joseph, his favorite son, from whom he once had been separated for a very long time. Jacob declared that Joseph was a fruitful vine by the spring. Even as a young boy, he had been promising and enterprising. He would bear much fruit because his place was by the spring. Jacob probably was referring here to Joseph's dependence on God—the only reason for him even staying alive and bearing fruit. It was only God who had refreshed Joseph during the difficult and trying situations he had faced.

Joseph's reliance on God had helped him cross over a wall and take the blessings of God to people outside his own borders. Jacob looked back to the time of the great famine and how, because Joseph had relied on God, God had given him the wisdom not only to provide for and preserve the people of Egypt, but also the many nations around them. Many families who lived outside Egypt, just as Jacob's did, survived the famine and were blessed because of Joseph.

Then Jacob quickly went on by referring to the fact that Joseph was attacked cruelly by many with much hate—an obvious reference to the way his own brothers detested him and even attempted to get rid of him, though Jacob may never have been aware of that incident. Jacob marveled at the way Joseph had stood strong and had held on, only because God held him in His very own hands and chose to bless him.

Notice that in his blessing, Jacob makes mention of three terms that describe this God whose hand was on Joseph's life. He called Him the Mighty One of Jacob, referring to His power; the Shepherd, because He is the One who guides; and the Rock of Israel, indicating that those who stand on Him will be firm and secure. This is the God who helped Joseph and blessed him, bestowing him with honor. This God would surely continue to bless him in every aspect of his life, with every kind of blessing.

Jacob concluded his prophecy over Joseph by reminding him that it was his privilege to receive blessings from his father, which definitely cannot be compared to any other kind of blessings or treasures. Then Jacob prayed that God's presence, His favor and His rich blessings would rest upon Joseph, "the prince among his brothers" (Genesis 49:26).

Jacob's rich words of blessing on Joseph also fell on Joseph's two sons, Ephraim and Manasseh. These two were, in fact, adopted by

Jacob (see Genesis 48:5), and eventually they replaced Joseph and Levi as tribes of Israel. When Joseph took his sons to Jacob, we read that Jacob chose to bless Ephraim before Manasseh, although Manasseh was the firstborn. When Joseph corrected him, Jacob replied, "I know, my son, I know. He too will become a people, and he too will become great. Nevertheless, his younger brother will be greater than he, and his descendants will become a group of nations" (Genesis 48:19).

The Tribes of Joseph's Sons

When we mention Joseph's descendants, it is important to keep in mind that a "tribe of Joseph" did not form as such. When Moses blessed the people who had descended from Joseph, he blessed the two tribes formed from Joseph's sons, Ephraim and Manasseh. Let's look at a little history about these two tribes that descended from the prince among his brothers, Joseph.

Like many of the other tribes, Ephraim disobeyed God by not expelling the Canaanites out of the land assigned to them (see Joshua 16:10). Later, during the time when Gideon fought with the Midianites, the Ephraimites were upset that Gideon did not call them when he went into battle. In fact, "they challenged him vigorously" about it (Judges 8:1). We see this tribe reacting in the same manner when Jephthah went to fight the Ammonites (Judges 12:1–2). Apparently, they did not like being left out of a fight. Sadly, this tribe that was called after Joseph (see Revelation 7:8) and received great blessings from Jacob, turned to the worship of Baal. God remembered their sin of idolatry: "The guilt of Ephraim is stored up, his sins are kept on record" (Hosea 13:12).

Although Jacob blessed Joseph's firstborn, Manasseh, after the secondborn, God did not forget Manasseh. One half of this tribe chose to settle on the east side of the Jordan River, along with the tribes of Reuben and Gad (see Numbers 32:33). The other half crossed the Jordan River and settled in the west (see Joshua 17:5–11).

They also assisted the other tribes that had crossed the Jordan River to conquer and possess the Promised Land, and they strengthened Gideon's hands against the Midianites (see Joshua 4:12; Judges 6; 7). During the reign of King Asa, many from the tribes of Ephraim and Manasseh seem to have settled in Judah because "they saw that the LORD his God was with him" (2 Chronicles 15:9). Some of those from these tribes that had settled in Jerusalem even returned from the Babylonian captivity (see 1 Chronicles 9:1–3). They recognized that the hand of God was with King Asa, and they chose to make Jerusalem their home. No wonder God preserved a remnant of faithful ones from both of these tribes.

Moses and the "Tribe of Joseph"

Moses had several things to say about Joseph and his descendants. As I said, rather than blessing a "tribe of Joseph," Moses actually was blessing the two tribes descended from the sons of Joseph, Ephraim and Manasseh. About these tribes he said,

> May the Lord bless his land with the precious dew from heaven above and with the deep waters that lie below; with the best the sun brings forth and the finest the moon can yield; with the choicest gifts of the ancient mountains and the fruitfulness of the everlasting hills; with the best gifts of the earth and its fullness and the favor of him who dwelt in the burning bush. Let all these rest on the head of Joseph, on the brow of the prince among his brothers. In majesty he is like a firstborn bull; his horns are the horns of a wild ox. With them he will gore the nations, even those at the ends of the earth. Such are the ten thousands of Ephraim; such are the thousands of Manasseh.
>
> Deuteronomy 33:13–17

The Message phrases it this way:

> Blessed by God be his land: the best fresh dew from high heaven, and fountains springing from the depths; the best radiance streaming

from the sun and the best the moon has to offer; beauty pouring off the tops of the mountains and the best from the everlasting hills; the best of Earth's exuberant gifts, the smile of the Burning-Bush Dweller. All this on the head of Joseph, on the brow of the consecrated one among his brothers. In splendor he's like a firstborn bull, his horns the horns of a wild ox; he'll gore the nations with those horns, push them all to the ends of the Earth. Ephraim by the ten thousands will do this, Manasseh by the thousands will do this.

The first part of Moses' words over Joseph are a reiteration of Jacob's words. He declares God's choicest blessings on Joseph, whom he also chose to call the prince among his brothers. Moses goes on to add that the very God who spoke to him from the burning bush would also shower Joseph's descendants with His favor.

Definitely, it was through God's favor that Joseph, the eleventh son of Jacob, received the birthright of the firstborn, which should have belonged to Reuben. That privilege was passed down to the two sons of Joseph, Ephraim and Manasseh (see 1 Chronicles 5:1). The rest of Moses' words focused on these two sons and what they would do in the future. They would be majestic and wild, and they would subdue nations both far and wide.

Moses agreed with Jacob that the best blessings must belong to Joseph, who deserved every one of them for holding on to his God. Joseph's sons would receive their portion of the firstborn's birthright as well. What an honor!

Today's Application for Us

The Bible contains numerous narratives about men and women of God who were blessed because they submitted to His plan in their lives. Let's look at some of these people whom God led to accomplish extraordinary things. Chapter 1 of the book of Esther begins the story of two of them, Mordecai and his cousin Esther, whom he adopted as a daughter. The story starts with King Xerxes. Angered by his wife's disobedience, King Xerxes banished Queen Vashti from his presence. He then began a search for a woman who could take the place of the queen. Beautiful maidens were brought from different parts of the kingdom, given beauty treatments in the palace for a year and then brought before the king. Esther, who "had a lovely figure and was beautiful," was brought to the palace as one of those maidens (Esther 2:7).

When Esther's turn came to go before the king, she found favor in his eyes and he chose her as his queen. This was God moving behind the scenes, placing Esther in the palace as an instrument in His hands for a specific purpose. Esther surely would have been unaware of this, of course.

Chapter 2 of Esther tells us that Mordecai revealed a plot to assassinate King Xerxes. Seated at the palace gates one day, Mordecai overheard two of the king's officers planning to kill the king. He informed Esther of this scheme, and she told the king. The conspirators were put to death, and a record of Mordecai's part in saving the king's life was written into the royal records. This, too, was God's hand working in the lives of Esther and Mordecai, preparing them to play a significant role in His master plan.

Chapter 3 tells us about Haman, an honored official in the kingdom, before whom everyone knelt to show their respect. As a Jew, Mordecai refused to yield to repeated entreaties to bow before Haman. He would bow before God, and before no other. Angered by Mordecai's seeming disrespect, Haman planned to kill the entire Jewish race. He carried false reports to the king, saying that the Jews had disobeyed the king's laws. King Xerxes granted him permission to destroy all the Jews in the kingdom. So fierce was Haman's anger against Mordecai that he also set up a fifty-cubit-high pole to impale Mordecai on (see Esther 5:14).

It is as true in our lives, as it was in Mordecai and Esther's, that even when things seem to be going terribly wrong, God is silently at work. He is ever-present and always in control. He took away King Xerxes's sleep one night, and as the chronicles of his reign were read to him, he was reminded of the service Mordecai had done him in uncovering the plot against his life. The king honored Mordecai the Jew the very next day (see Esther 6).

After much fasting and prayer, and at the risk of her life, Esther revealed to King Xerxes the cruel plot Haman had put together against her people. Justice was carried out as the furious king ordered his men to impale Haman on the very pole that the man had prepared for Mordecai. The Jews were also given permission to arm and defend themselves, and God's chosen people were saved from being completely wiped out that day. The plan of God for their protection was beautifully carried out through two lives that were lived in submission to Him.

Jesus' life on earth was lived fully in submission to the will of the Father. He left His heavenly glory, took on the form of man and humbled Himself, even to death on the cross (see Philippians 2:6–8). Even as a young boy of twelve, Jesus knew what His purpose was in life. He knew what His Father wanted Him to do (see Luke 2:41–49). There were numerous times during His ministry when people spoke against Him, found fault with Him, accused Him and scorned Him, but He kept His eyes fixed on the purpose that had been laid out for His life. He had come to the world to die for the sins of mankind, and He let nothing distract Him from this heavenly task.

The Pharisees and Sadducees of Jesus' time, the hypocritical religious leaders who could never agree with each other, found that one thing they could agree on and join together for was criticizing Jesus. Jealous of His tremendous influence over the people, they tried to humiliate Him at every opportunity and discredit Him before the crowds who thronged around Him. They even went to the extent of saying that Jesus cast out demons by the power of Beelzebub, the prince of demons (see Matthew 12:22–24).

These jealous religious leaders finally succeeded in having Jesus crucified. Even when He was hanging on the cross, however, as the innocent Lamb of God suffering for our sins, those around Him insulted and taunted Him. Jesus has all the power in heaven and earth; He could have come down from the cross and destroyed those who ridiculed Him. But He endured the suffering because of the joy set before Him (see Hebrews 12:2). Jesus is alive today, exalted above every name, all authority in His hand, seated at the right hand of the Father. His sufferings opened the way to heaven for us. Because He followed the Father's plan, we are blessed.

God's Hand Is Always There

I have been through many trying situations over the years, but God has always been there for me. I remember the time when we were raising funds for our church building. Key leaders of the organization I belong to promised that they would match equally whatever amount I raised in my church. I went on a long fast and challenged my congregation one Sunday to give liberally toward the building project. We took an offering and collected pledges at the end of the service. We received Indian rupees 3 lakh in cash (about $20,000 then, with each lakh being Indian rupees 100,000) and pledges that amounted to Indian rupees 19 lakh (about $126,667). I let my organization know the amount that had been collected and pledged, and they in turn agreed to match the amount. With great excitement, we began our construction work at the site God had given us.

We used all the money we had on hand to buy building materials. I wanted our church to have a basement, too, so we had to dig to a depth of twelve to fifteen feet. We had no money to hire a bulldozer for this work, but I got a demolisher to come tear down the house that was on the site. He gave me Indian rupees 35,000 (about $2,333 then) for the materials he salvaged after the demolition, and with this money we dug the ground for the basement. The church members kept giving money, but it went out as fast as it came in. The foundational work had started. I was working more than fifteen hours a day at the site, and the building was taking shape.

One day, the key leaders who had promised the matching money suddenly called me. The person in charge of our church accounts prepared an audited report of the expenses incurred thus far in the construction. I took a copy for each of the leaders and went to meet with them. Eagerly I gave them each a copy, but they all laid the copies aside without even glancing at them and told me they had something they wanted to say. Someone who was not happy at seeing my ministry being blessed had antagonized them against me. They informed me of their decision not to support the construction work financially.

I was deeply shaken by their announcement. The leaders gave me a chance to speak for myself. Instead of venting my anger on them, I only said, "God has given me a vision to build this church. Even if I have to go through struggles, I will stay strong and build it. If God has chosen that I should suffer at your hands, then I will suffer."

With a broken heart I came out of our meeting at around 8:45 p.m., and I held on to a jackfruit tree that was nearby and cried my heart out. I got into my car in a daze and drove straight to the construction site. I asked the watchman for a chair and I sat there for two hours, crying out to God so intensely that I did not even notice my chair sinking into the mud.

What's happening, God? I questioned Him. *What will I tell the people in the church?*

His reassuring reply came to me: *Just tell them the truth.* God then asked me, *What have you given for the building work?*

My whole life is for the ministry, Lord! I replied.

Turn around, He told me.

I did so, and there I saw my Ambassador car, which I cherished very much.

Sell it and give the money for the building, God said.

That Sunday the title of my sermon was "One Thing I Have Desired Is to Serve My Master." I told the congregation of my decision to sell my car and give the money for the building. The entire congregation was touched; there was not one dry eye in the place. One person came forward to buy my car. The next day, with tears in my eyes I exchanged that car for a check for Indian rupees 75,000 (about $5,000 then) and sowed the money into the Kingdom of God.

"Even if the leaders do not support you, we will support you," the people assured me that day. "We will build the church together, Pastor."

The people gave their gold jewelry and sold their property to contribute toward the building. With the support of the church members and many other missionary friends of mine, in just seven months we completed the construction of the church.

People have tried constantly to sabotage my life and ministry, but God has always been there, protecting, providing and proving His faithfulness. I recall another incident that occurred in the initial stages of my ministry. There were just 29 people in the church then, and on Sundays I used to say while preaching, "God will give me the biggest church in Bangalore!"

One Sunday a group of seven people from the congregation came up to me and said, "Listen to us, you are young. You don't know what you are saying. Don't keep saying you will have the biggest church in Bangalore. You are embarrassing us. If you repeat it again, we will surely leave the church."

That week I spent much time in fasting and prayer. The next Sunday I went up to preach and again said, "God will give me the biggest church in Bangalore!"

The seven people who had warned me came up to me again and said, "We are leaving the church."

I did not ask them to stay. I just said, "See you in heaven." Then some years ago, long after that early incident, I went to invite them to my son's wedding. They were shocked to see me and told me that they deeply regretted the words they had spoken all those years back.

Even though people have tried hard to stop my God-given vision, I put my trust in God, focused on my vision and kept going. I have always felt God's hand on my life as He helped me rise above every problem and soar high like an eagle for Him.

Ways to Live a Life of Surrender

God never changes; He is the Rock on whom we can stand firm, trusting Him to carry us through each and every situation. If we were to live our lives or build our ministry trusting people, we would be sure to meet with failure, heartbreak and pain. But when our lives, family and ministry are built on God, they are sure to flourish with His blessings. Here are some pointers we can follow to live a life in complete surrender to the Master:

Fear God and walk with Him in times of adversity. Jesus does not tell us that our Christian lives will be completely trouble free. Rather, He tells us that most definitely, we will encounter troubles, yet we are to trust in Him: "In this world you will have trouble. But take heart! I have overcome the world" (John 16:33). As we begin to fear God and walk in the path He has chosen for us, His presence hems us in "behind and before," and His hand is on us (Psalm 139:5). We can walk boldly through any kind of situation, assured of our Master's presence leading the way.

Fall at the feet of the Master in total dependence. When problems and trials come our way, instead of turning immediately to the limited problem-solving abilities of friends and loved ones, let's learn to take our troubles to the infinite wisdom of our Master. "It is better to take refuge in the Lord than to trust in humans" (Psalm 118:8). As we surrender our lives and impossible situations at His feet and ask Him to take complete control, He will take over and do the impossible in our lives. Just as David strengthened himself in the Lord when his own men turned against him, let's find our strength and hope in God alone (see 1 Samuel 30:6).

Follow the direction of the Spirit of the Lord. Let's learn to be sensitive to the Holy Spirit, who dwells within us. Even though God had destined Joseph for greatness, he suffered for many years. Yet he was always sensitive to the presence of God, who was with him and who guided him through every adverse situation (see Genesis 39:2). The book of Acts says the apostle Paul and his companions followed the direction of the Holy Spirit throughout their travels (see Acts 16:6–8). We must do the same on our spiritual journey. As we take our troubles to God in prayer and tell Him that we depend on Him alone, the Holy Spirit will give us the divine wisdom to act in the particular situations we encounter.

Face difficult situations, knowing that God will deliver you. As children of the Most High God, we do not run away in fear from troubles; we face them boldly, knowing that our God is in control. "The righteous are as bold as a lion" (Proverbs 28:1). Innumerable times in the Bible, God has told us to call on Him in the day of trouble and He will rescue us. With the knowledge that "God is not human, that he should lie" (Numbers 23:19), we can meet any situation that comes our way, knowing that victory is ours.

Focus on the call of God in your life. There is a specific, God-ordained purpose for each and every one of our lives in this world. We need to focus on the dream, the vision that God has placed in our lives, and run toward it without letting anything tempt us or distract us away from it. Let's always fix our eyes on Jesus, the Author and Perfecter of our faith, and always "run with perseverance" this earthly race God has marked out for us (Hebrews 12:1–2). As the apostle Paul says, "Run in such a way as to get the prize" (1 Corinthians 9:24).

As we spend time in the presence of God, hold on to Him at all times and surrender our lives to live for the fulfillment of His divine purpose for us, He will prove a Friend faithful and true, constant in our sorrows and joys. When we recognize His hand in our lives, as did Joseph and the others we have talked about, God will lift us up and bless us beyond anything we have ever imagined.

Let's Pray Together

Heavenly Father, thank You for Your faithfulness. We have placed You at the helm of our lives. We choose to follow Your Word in times of blessing and in times of adversity. We bow before You and give You complete control.

You are our hope and our salvation. We will be sensitive to the guidance of the Holy Spirit. We will be still and listen for Your voice and Your guidance. Embolden us to face the struggles in our lives. Pour over us the blessings of Joseph, so that we, too, may trust in You and overcome.

You have called us out, restored us and equipped us to live for You. We want to live our lives in Your presence and fulfill Your divine plan for us.

In Jesus' name we pray, Amen.

12

Benjamin

Happy are those who rest secure in God,
for they will enjoy constant fellowship and shelter.

The path the Lord led me through as this ministry was being built was filled with struggles, but He has always been there with me. As I pause and look back now, I stand in awe when I see the great and marvelous works His hands have done. We dedicated our church building on December 18, 1994, and when we started having services in it, we were a crowd of 400 people. The church grew rapidly, and soon we felt the need to add a balcony to accommodate the overflowing crowds. We had a "Miracle 7 Lakh" Sunday to raise money to build the balcony. Our God, who blesses us exceedingly and abundantly, above all that we ever ask of Him, enabled us to raise all that and more—7 lakhs and another 50,000 rupees—and we built the balcony. It has been 22 years since we moved into our church building. As a result of prayer, fasting, hard work and God-given strategies, this church, which began with just 3 people, has grown to more than 25,000 people today. Truly, we serve a God of wonders.

It is my heart's desire that the nations around us should also experience the abundant blessings God has showered upon us. Our church has built more than 300 churches and bought more than 100 properties for building churches in the countries of India, Nepal, Sri Lanka and the border areas of Bhutan. In Nepal alone, we built 75 churches for the glory of God. The state where we are situated is a hard place for ministries to grow. As a result, God has placed a burden in my heart for the many pastors who are doing the Lord's work amidst tough situations. As a church we fasted and prayed for ten days, and then one Sunday we raised money to support these pastors. That Sunday morning, we raised 4.5 crores. (Each crore equals 10 million rupees, so we raised the equivalent of about $682,000 in today's dollars.) This money was not in pledges, but in actual cash. We also gifted pieces of land to 105 pastors, and we are partnering with different ministries to build churches on those properties.

The building we are in at present is in no way sufficient to accommodate the more than 25,000 people who attend our services, so we decided to buy another larger piece of land so that we can grow to 50,000 people. After 7 months of fasting and prayer, we appointed a particular Sunday for our fund-raising and held a single service at a huge venue that we rent for large services. The people gave joyfully and generously; it took them an hour and 50 minutes to come to the front and give their money, land and jewels. We even had the facility set up for people to give by swiping their cards. By the end of the day, we had raised almost 15 crores (or about $2.2 million today). That was a day of celebrating God's goodness! More than 30,000 people came, gave their best to God, partook of a fellowship lunch and went back home happily. We are praying and waiting in faith for the next step; God is very soon going to take us to our next miracle land.

I often say, "I am a soldier of Jesus; I am restless till I rest in the arms of Jesus!" I do not let fatigue or troubles stop me from working for the Master. His presence is my constant guide, my comfort when I am low and my defense when enemies arise. Those who rest secure in Him find fellowship and shelter, as the Israelites found out at many points throughout their history. Exodus chapters 7–12 recount the ten plagues that the Lord sent down on Egypt, through which He revealed His power and might to the pharaoh who refused to let His people go. In spite of suffering severely because of the first nine plagues, Egypt's pharaoh still stubbornly refused to yield to God's command. In Exodus 11 God revealed to Moses the tenth and worst plague that He would send on the Egyptians: He was going to kill every firstborn male child in Egypt, from the king's heir to the firstborn son of the poorest in the land. The Israelites, God's chosen people, would be safe, however, in the land of Goshen where they dwelt.

God commanded that each household among the Israelites slaughter a one-year-old lamb and apply its blood on the sides and tops of the door frames of their houses. He promised, "The blood will be a sign for you on the houses where you are, and when I see the blood, I will pass over you. No destructive plague will touch you when I strike Egypt" (Exodus 12:13). The Israelites were safe under the wings of Yahweh, secure in His promise to protect them. God did as He had promised; there was wailing throughout the land of Egypt as the Egyptians lost their firstborn sons, but the Israelites were unharmed. Let's look at a few more verses from the Bible about the safety and respite we have in the presence of the Lord:

> Then the LORD will create over all of Mount Zion and over those who assemble there a cloud of smoke by day and a glow of flaming fire by night; over everything the glory will be a canopy. It will be a shelter and shade from the heat of the day, and a refuge and hiding place from the storm and rain.
>
> Isaiah 4:5–6

> He will hide me in the shelter of his sacred tent and set me high upon a rock.
>
> Psalm 27:5

Whoever fears the LORD has a secure fortress, and for their children it will be a refuge.

Proverbs 14:26

The name of the LORD is a fortified tower; the righteous run to it and are safe.

Proverbs 18:10

Come with me by yourselves to a quiet place and get some rest.

Mark 6:31

In Genesis 49, Jacob compares his youngest son, Benjamin, to a ravenous wolf, a hungry wild beast successful in its hunt. Moses' prophecy over Benjamin, on the other hand, strikes a completely different note. His prophecy describes the tribe of Benjamin as the beloved of the Lord, secure and at rest in Him.

The presence of the Lord is a place of peace, quiet and rest. It is a place where we receive divine strength and guidance; it is a place of miracles and wonders. Let's resolve in our hearts to sit at the Lord's feet every day and be renewed by the warmth and strength that flows from His throne. May our faces reflect His glory.

The Birth of Benjamin

Much had taken place after the birth of Rachel's firstborn son, Joseph, Benjamin's only full-blood brother. Jacob had deceived his father-in-law, Laban, and had fled from him. Laban had then pursued Jacob, and after a confrontation they parted in peace (see Genesis 30–31). Further, Jacob had decided to return to Esau, his brother, from whom he had deceptively taken away the birthright. Fearing what Esau's response might be at their first meeting, Jacob sent his servants ahead with many gifts to pacify his brother. To Jacob's relief, their reunion went favorably. In the meantime, God had dealt with Jacob and had changed his name from Jacob to Israel (see Genesis 32–33).

We talked in chapters 2 and 3 about how Jacob's sons Simeon and Levi had taken matters into their own hands at Shechem, where their sister, Dinah, was defiled. These two sons treacherously slaughtered every man in that city and plundered it (see Genesis 34). On God's direction Jacob returned to Bethel after that, first purifying his entire household. God made a covenant with Jacob that the land He had given to Abraham and Isaac, He would give to Jacob as well (see Genesis 35). Through all these events, we see no trace of any further struggle between Leah and Rachel for Jacob's love or for more children. Apparently, their sibling rivalry had ceased as both Leah and Rachel matured over time.

Jacob and his household moved on from Bethel to Ephrath while Rachel was pregnant with her second child. As they were nearing Ephrath, she went into such a difficult labor that it took her life, but not before she had given birth to Benjamin and had named him:

> While they were still some distance from Ephrath, Rachel began to give birth and had great difficulty. And as she was having great difficulty in childbirth, the midwife said to her, "Don't despair, for you have another son." As she breathed her last—for she was dying—she named her son Ben-Oni. But his father named him Benjamin.
>
> Genesis 35:16–18

With no strength left as her life ebbed away, Rachel named her son Ben-Oni, which we are told means "son of my trouble." Not wanting his son to be known by that name as he grew up, however, Jacob chose to rename the boy Benjamin, which we are told means "son of my right hand." During Joseph's birth previously, Rachel had asked God to give her this second son. Her desire had been fulfilled, but Benjamin's birth brought upon her great trouble and left Jacob heartbroken over the death of his favorite wife. Yet Jacob chose to draw strength from the birth of this son, born to him while he was well advanced in years. Benjamin was the son on whom he could lean, the son of his right hand. To Jacob, the birth of Benjamin signified strength in his old age.

Benjamin in the Joseph Narrative

Three things stand out in relation to Benjamin and his family. In regard to his father, Jacob, Benjamin took the place of his long-lost brother, Joseph. Imagine the sorrow that must have overtaken Jacob when Joseph had gone missing and was presumed dead. The lively memory of Joseph must have been so fresh in Jacob's mind, but alas, the boy was with them no more. All the fatherly love he had lavished on Joseph, Jacob now lavished on Benjamin. He would not even let the boy out of his sight (see Genesis 42:4, 36–38; 43:6–14; 44:30–31).

In regard to Benjamin's brothers, we are quick to notice their changed mentality. Compared to the manner in which they had treated their brother Joseph and sold him as a slave, they were totally transformed. The very same brothers now took care of their brother Benjamin. They stood up for him and were willing to risk their lives to protect him at all costs (see Genesis 42:21–22, 37; 43:8–9; 44:18–34).

Finally, in regard to his blood brother, Joseph, Benjamin was also greatly loved. It deeply moved Joseph when he heard his older brothers speak of their "youngest brother" still at home. Naturally, he wanted to see Benjamin for himself, so he ordered them to bring the boy back to Egypt with them. When his brothers finally managed to bring Benjamin along, look at Joseph's response when they met:

> As he looked about and saw his brother Benjamin, his own mother's son, he asked, "Is this your youngest brother, the one you told me about?" And he said, "God be gracious to you, my son." Deeply moved at the sight of his brother, Joseph hurried out and looked for a place to weep. He went into his private room and wept there.
>
> Genesis 43:29–30

Later, when food was served, Joseph gave five times more to Benjamin than to the others (see Genesis 43:34). And when he revealed his identity to his family, he proudly acknowledged Benjamin as "my brother" (Genesis 45:12).

Benjamin was greatly loved by his father, Jacob, fiercely protected by his older brothers and happily reunited with his own blood brother, Joseph.

Jacob's Prophetic Words over Benjamin

After Jacob had pronounced great blessings on Joseph, he then looked on Joseph's full brother, Benjamin, the youngest of them all and the son born when Jacob was so advanced in age. As every other father would have, Jacob must have desired to declare good things over this precious son. But carried by the Spirit of God, Jacob saw that Benjamin would become dangerous in the future—very dangerous:

> Benjamin is a ravenous wolf; in the morning he devours the prey, in the evening he divides the plunder.
>
> Genesis 49:27

The Message phrases it as,

> Benjamin is a ravenous wolf; all morning he gorges on his kill, at evening divides up what's left over.

Jacob referred to the "son of his right hand" as a famished, hungry wolf, wild and desperate. This wolf would greedily attack his prey and selfishly consume it till he had had enough. And after he had gotten all he wanted, then he would choose to split up what was left over. In other words, Jacob was saying that Benjamin could not be controlled and that in his selfishness, he would do whatever he chose.

The Benjamites and the Judges

Benjamin's descendants went on to fulfill the prophecy Jacob had spoken over their forefather. Many of them were indeed a fierce, wild people who followed their own desires, although eventually, as we will see, some great individuals would arise from among them. During the time of Israel's judges, the Benjamites failed to drive out the Jebusites from the portion of the land assigned to them, in clear disobedience of God's command (see Judges 1:21). The Benjamite Ehud, however, had no such failings. He was a judge whom God raised up to fight against the Moabites, who were oppressing the people of Israel: "Again the Israelites cried out to the LORD, and he gave them a deliverer—Ehud, a left-handed man, the son of Gera the Benjamite. The Israelites sent him with tribute to Eglon king of Moab" (Judges 3:15). With a sword in his left hand, Ehud single-handedly put to death the king of Moab and led the Israelites in victory against the Moabites (see verses 16–30).

In Deborah's song of victory over the Canaanites, which we talked about earlier, the judge Deborah makes a fleeting remark about the fact that men from Benjamin had come to help in the battle, though she mentions nothing else outstanding about them (see Judges 5:14). The book of Judges also describes an appalling incident that took place involving the Benjamites. The narrative revolves around a Levite who, along with his concubine, was traveling back to their home in the hill country of Ephraim. Not wanting to spend the night in Jebus since the people there were not Israelites, this Levite took his concubine to Gibeah in the territory of the Benjamites. Mistakenly, he was convinced it would be better and safer for them there (see Judges 19:11–13).

Sadly, once they reached Gibeah no one bothered about them. As evening approached, an elderly man, an Ephraimite who happened to stay in Gibeah, saw them in the city square. Warning them not to spend the night there, he took them into his home. But even his kind act could not protect them. The tragic events of that night eventually led to the concubine being defiled and left for dead by the Benjamites from Gibeah. The Levite brought her body home, cut it into twelve parts and sent the parts to the twelve tribes (see Judges 19:14–30). Horrified, all of Israel got together in response and decided to deal with the Benjamites from Gibeah. They first asked that the guilty men be handed over to them, but the Benjamites would not respond:

> The Benjamites would not listen to their fellow Israelites. From their towns they came together at Gibeah to fight against the Israelites. At once the Benjamites mobilized twenty-six thousand swordsmen from their towns, in addition to seven hundred able young men from those living in Gibeah. Among all these soldiers there were seven hundred select troops who were left-handed, each of whom could sling a stone at a hair and not miss.
>
> Judges 20:13–16

The trained warriors among the Benjamites readied themselves to fight their brother tribes. To oppose them, "Israel, apart from Benjamin, mustered four hundred thousand swordsmen, all of them fit for battle" (Judges 20:17). The fighting was intense, and initially the other tribes of Israel seemed to be losing ground against the Benjamites. But they cried out to the Lord, who had directed them to oppose the Benjamites for their evil actions. The Israelites sought God's favor, and on His direction they attacked again. God defeated the Benjamites, who had only six hundred fighting men left at the end of the battle. These few ran for their lives (see verses 18–48). The Israelites then grieved that such a disaster should overtake their brothers, and they cried, "Today one tribe is cut off from Israel" (Judges 21:6).

With all the other tribes taking an oath before the Lord that they would not give their daughters in marriage to the Benjamites, it may have seemed as if everything were over for the tribe of Benjamin (see Judges 21:7, 18). But it was not over yet. Seeing that the number of Benjamites who remained alive was small, the rest of the tribes made other provisions for them to ensure that they were able to take wives and have heirs. The Benjamites then returned to their inheritance, rebuilt the towns and settled in them (see verses 12–24).

The Benjamites and the Kings

In 1 Samuel 8 we read that one day the people of Israel approached the prophet Samuel and asked him for a king to lead them, since he was growing old. They wanted to have a king rule over them, as the nations around them did. Samuel took their request to God, and God told him to warn the people about what kings ruling over them would do to them. Samuel attempted to make the people realize how their choice to have a king would one day fill them with regret. Nevertheless, the Israelites did not budge and still demanded a king. The very first king God chose and had Samuel anoint was Saul, a Benjamite:

> There was a Benjamite, a man of standing, whose name was Kish son of Abiel, the son of Zeror, the son of Becorath, the son of Aphiah of Benjamin. He had a son named Saul, an impressive young man without equal among the Israelites—a head taller than any of the others.
>
> 1 Samuel 9:1–2 NIV1984

Saul is an example of a Benjamite who started out well, but ended in total disaster due to his headstrong ways. Initially, Saul relied on God and did extremely well as king of Israel. But little by little he drifted away from God, took matters into his own hands and disobeyed God, earning a strong rebuke from Samuel (see 1 Samuel 15:22–23). Saul chose not to humble himself in repentance before God, so eventually he had to make way for David, of the tribe of Judah, to succeed him as king (see 1 Samuel 16:1–13). Saul stirred God's wrath against him so much that "the Spirit of the LORD had departed from Saul, and an evil spirit from the LORD tormented him" (verse 14). This impressive Benjamite did not make the best use of the power God granted him, and he lost his opportunity to be king.

Many Benjamites from King Saul's side chose to defect to David's side. These men were once again described in Scripture as able warriors, trained for battle and perfect in their aim: "They were armed with bows and were able to shoot arrows or to sling stones right-handed or left-handed; they were relatives of Saul from the tribe of Benjamin" (1 Chronicles 12:2). It is amazing that they could aim with either of their hands, yet not miss. These were the kind of men who stood with David and helped him greatly. Later, the Bible again describes them as valiant soldiers and brave fighting men (see 2 Chronicles 14:8; 17:17–18).

The Bible also mentions some other remarkable people from the tribe of Benjamin. Two of them are Mordecai and Esther, whose story we talked about in chapter 11. They saved the Jewish people from annihilation at the hands of Haman. The great apostle Paul himself was a Benjamite whom God chose for the purpose of carrying the Gospel to the Gentiles (see Romans 11:1; Philippians 3:5). From the very Benjamite tribe who had earlier incurred the wrath of God and the judgment of Israel came these individuals who submitted to God and obediently followed Him.

Moses and the Tribe of Benjamin

While Jacob probably got a prophetic glimpse into the evil act of the Benjamites at Gibeah and described them as wolves out to kill, Moses sees the blessing that will come forth from Benjamin. About Benjamin and his tribe, Moses says,

> Let the beloved of the LORD rest secure in him, for he shields him all day long, and the one the LORD loves rests between his shoulders.
>
> Deuteronomy 33:12

The Message says it this way:

> GOD's beloved; GOD's permanent residence. Encircled by GOD all day long, within whom GOD is at home.

Moses chooses to call Benjamin "God's beloved." What a difference from the ravenous wolf Jacob had called him, yet both Jacob and Moses are referring to the same person. Benjamin may have been the son of his father's right hand and a wolf, according to Jacob. But more than that, Moses says, Benjamin and his descendants will be ones greatly loved of God.

As a child finds peace and security in the arms of his father, so also will Benjamin and his tribe enjoy calm even in the midst of a storm. How can Benjamin be at rest? Moses is quick to explain that Benjamin's rest comes from the fact that he will be surrounded by God's mighty presence. God will cover him, shield him, shelter him and protect him, not just for a brief moment during the day, but throughout the entire day. What else could Benjamin and his descendants need?

Moses further prophetically declares that God will make His home within Benjamin. How true this would be. King David desired to build a place in which the presence of God would dwell, and as a result the Temple was finally built and dedicated by his son, King Solomon, according to the plan of God. That Temple was built in the territory of the Benjamites—Jerusalem (see 1 Chronicles 22; Psalm 68:29).

What a change had come over the tribe of Benjamin. They became the light to Judah that was never to be put out (see 1 Kings 11:36). They remained a blessing to Judah.

Today's Application for Us

The assurance that God gives is far better than the best securities that this world can offer. It reminds me of a story in the Bible about a woman who chose to rest secure in God and found abundant fellowship and shelter. In fact, she found a whole new life. The book of Ruth paints a beautiful picture of this woman, Ruth the Moabitess. She married a man from Bethlehem who had come to live in Moab because of the famine in Bethlehem. About ten years after their marriage, Ruth lost her husband.

In the meantime, Naomi, her mother-in-law, became dejected and bitter because she had lost her husband first, and soon after that lost both her sons. Hearing that the famine was no longer a problem in Judah, she decided to return there. Though Naomi tried to persuade both her daughters-in-law to stay in their Moabite homeland, only Orpah went back home and did not accompany Naomi. Ruth, however, was determined to stay with her mother-in-law. She did not allow anything Naomi said to discourage her from going along. She told Naomi, "Don't urge me to leave you or to turn back from you. Where you go I will go, and where you stay I will stay. Your people will be my people and your God my God" (Ruth 1:16).

Ruth chose to be faithful to her mother-in-law and also follow Naomi's God. She treated her mother-in-law with kindness and took care of her. In return, she enjoyed the favor of God. Once the two women were back in Bethlehem, Ruth decided to glean leftover grain from the fields. God granted her favor in the eyes of one field's owner, Boaz, who happened to be a close relative of Naomi's. He not only treated Ruth well, but also made sure there was a good quantity of grain left over for her to collect. He further instructed his workers to treat her well.

The Bible goes on to tell us that Boaz redeemed Ruth and married her. The women of Bethlehem gave Ruth credit, telling Naomi that clearly her daughter-in-law loved her and was better to her than seven sons (see Ruth 4:15). Ruth went to collect grain from a field, but God gave her the field. He gave her Boaz, who became her kinsman redeemer and husband. They had a child and named him Obed, and Obed became the father of Jesse, the father of King David.

Ruth, an ordinary Moabite woman, became secure in God, for He became her shelter. She entrusted Him with her future. In return, she enjoyed a privilege that only a few other women in history have—her name was entered in the genealogy of Jesus Christ, for He was a descendant of King David. Ruth became a blessing by trusting God and resting in His comfort.

Jesus is our ultimate Source of comfort. The security that the world can offer us will slowly fade away, till we are left with nothing. But even then, Jesus welcomes us with arms wide open, saying, "Come to me, all you who are weary and burdened, and I will give you rest. Take my yoke upon you and learn from me, for I am gentle and humble in heart, and you will find rest for your souls. For my yoke is easy and my burden is light" (Matthew 11:28–30).

The New Testament depicts Timothy as being like a son to the apostle Paul, who was very fond of him. While writing Timothy a letter, Paul said, "I am reminded of your sincere faith, which first lived in your grandmother Lois and in your mother Eunice and, I am persuaded, now lives in you also" (2 Timothy 1:5). Paul commended Timothy for the faith that could be seen in three generations of his family. He encouraged Timothy to follow in his footsteps and rely on God. He also gave Timothy one particular instruction: "And the things you have heard me say in the presence of many witnesses entrust to reliable people who will also be qualified to teach others" (2 Timothy 2:2). He goes on to say, "But as for you, continue in what you have learned and have become convinced of, because you know those from whom you learned it" (2 Timothy 3:14).

The apostle Paul wanted Timothy to stay strong in the faith and in what he had learned. While the storms around us aim at deviating us from our course, our only security is in God and in His strength. It is during such times that our foundation becomes evident and its strength is revealed. Few have faced as many stormy times as Paul, yet even though he was in prison, he still encouraged Timothy—and all of us—to rely on God.

The apostle Paul's words to Timothy remind us not only that faith can be seen from one generation to the next, but also that we need to ensure that we teach reliable people, who will in turn teach others. Reliable people who have their trust in God will always turn toward God when in need of shelter. Our comfort comes not from this world, but from God. As the psalmist says, "In peace I will lie down and sleep, for you alone, LORD, make me dwell in safety" (Psalm 4:8).

"Prayer Penetration"

It is my heart's desire to see India washed by the blood of the Lamb. I often tell God, *Give me no name; give me no fame. Give me souls for India to be saved!* It was while I was praying this that God put a burden in my heart to travel all over India and other nations and pray for revival to break out across the globe. My mission was to meet pastors and challenge them into leadership and a ministry of prayer. It takes a pastor to know the feelings of a pastor. Most of us go through difficult situations where we have no support and only God sees our tears. God started to speak words of life and comfort into those situations through "Prayer Penetration," the ministry that came out of my burden and prayer.

Prayer Penetration is a ministry that God placed in my heart in which we take prayer drives from one place to another. I told you a little bit about it at the start of chapter 10, but I want to tell you more about how so many have found fellowship and shelter through it as God has expanded it into many more places. On our Prayer Penetration drives we pray, claim the victory of Christ, break the powers of the enemy and through the power of the Holy Spirit set people free. We first drove from Jammu and Kashmir (the northern end of India) to Kanyakumari (the southern end of India), praying for revival in all those places. After that, I took a 38-member team to Sri Lanka, where we went from one place to another, praying and breaking strongholds.

My burden was not only for India, but for other nations as well. Led by the Holy Spirit, I conducted Prayer Penetrations in Bhutan, Burma, Bangladesh, Nepal, Singapore and Malaysia. I still have maps that show the routes we traveled in all these places.

After traveling and praying throughout India and the surrounding SAARC (South Asian Association for Regional Cooperation) countries, God opened the doors for me to conduct prayer drives abroad in places like Sydney and Melbourne, Australia, and Auckland, New Zealand. I did not want to keep the joy and anointing that we had for our church alone. We wanted to be a blessing to many people.

God then enabled me to pray, bless and break the strongholds in the seven emirates of the UAE (the United Arab Emirates)— Abu Dhabi, Dubai, Sharjah, Ras Al Khaimah, Ajman, Umm Al Quwain and Fujairah. It was not easy, but we did not give up. We kept pressing on. I went to Gujarat (in Western India) during a time of severe persecution. I met the pastors and leaders there and encouraged them. It was there that God impressed these words upon my heart: *My passion, vision and compassion make me to go beyond my limitations.*

My next mission was to pray for Europe. I traveled with my son, Roger Samuel, and his wife, Nicole, along with a pastor friend. We went to 22 countries in Europe and prayed for a mighty outpouring of the Holy Spirit. We hired a car and drove to all those countries. In each place that we went, we would park in a downtown area of a city and then walk for hours, praying for that nation. We would then return to the vehicle, turn on the GPS and head to the next nation. Physically weary but spiritually fiery, we did not allow anything to hinder us from praying.

At one point in our journey, we traveled to eight countries in ten days. We drove five thousand kilometers by car and prayed over England, France, Holland, Belgium, Germany, Switzerland, Italy and Luxembourg. We prayed for God to send a revival. In certain places we faced opposition and were denied entry, but that did not stop us. We also went to Norway, Sweden, Germany, Denmark, Finland, Poland, the Czech Republic, Slovakia, Hungary, Romania, Serbia, Croatia, Slovenia and Austria. We drove through all those places and prayed that the people would be saved, the churches would grow and the pastors would minister with a new burden and with fire.

During one of my Prayer Penetration drives in Maharashtra, I went to a place called Basmath. There was heavy opposition there against the prayer drive. We had scheduled a time to conduct prayer in a certain hall, but some of our opposition threatened the owners and instructed them not to give us the hall. The owners of our hotel were also threatened and told that they would be harmed if they allowed us to stay. At one point, I noticed ten men ready and waiting to attack me. The pastor I was with then took me to a paddy field, where I had to speak to the people who had assembled there. After challenging the leaders and pastors, I got into the van to leave and saw those ten men blocking the road. I knew that in two minutes I would be dead! Immediately, I breathed out two things to God: I asked Him to take care of my family, and I asked Him to wash India in the blood of Jesus. As we moved forward, out of confusion those ten men moved out of the way because they thought I was in another bus. God confused the plans of the enemy and helped us get back unharmed. Last year, the same man who led the opposition gave his heart to the Lord and is now a believer.

Challenges neither weakened my faith nor put out the fire inside me. I conducted Prayer Penetrations in Toronto, the Fiji Islands and Mauritius. From a small beginning with three people, God has used us in amazing ways to touch many nations through prayer. Despite trials and opposition, we always forged ahead, praying and preaching in the churches before we moved on to the next place. Through it all, I was convinced that this was what God wanted us to do and that it would bless people. We did not limit God. Though our beginning was tough, in 34 years God has enabled me to travel to and pray for 64 nations. He also has enabled me to conduct Power Conferences that more than 181,000 pastors and leaders have attended, training them to rise up, serve and take their churches to the next level.

Ways to Rest Secure in God

We have seen many examples from the Bible and from the Benjamites of the blessings that can result from resting secure in God. Here are five lessons that I have learned through my experiences in life about resting secure in Him. These lessons can guide us to surrender everything to our heavenly Father and see the fullness of His blessings in our lives and ministry:

Look for fields ripe for harvest. Genesis 13 says that Abraham's nephew Lot looked at the lush, green Jordan Valley and chose to dwell there. The Bible tells us that Lot first sat at the gate of the sinful city of Sodom, but soon entered the city (see Genesis 19). In doing that, he let the city enter his heart. He chose the place based on his human understanding. He chose what his human perception said was good, but it did not result in blessings. Unlike Lot, let's look at the fields that are ripe for harvest, not at places that look prosperous or comfortable to us. Let's look at the places where Jesus is needed. Jesus said, "I tell you, open your eyes and look at the fields! They are ripe for harvest" (John 4:35). Abraham looked to God, and he was blessed. Through him the nations of the world have been blessed. Though the ministry fields may seem hard, let's choose to stay in the place where God has placed us.

Labor without expectations. The work we do for our Master is not for earthly gain or riches, nor for fame and fortune. We do His work so that perishing souls will be saved. Our ultimate reward comes from Him. Externally we may perish, but internally we grow strong. This physical body ages and wears away, but our spirit goes from strength to strength as we pour ourselves out in the service of Jesus. As the apostle Paul said, "What is more, I consider everything a loss because of the surpassing worth of knowing Christ Jesus my Lord, for whose sake I have lost all things. I consider them garbage, that I may gain Christ" (Philippians 3:8). No material gain in this world should ever be able to distract us from living our lives for God.

Learn to lean on God. Terrified because Queen Jezebel had threatened to murder him, Elijah ran for his life. When he reached Mount Horeb, he entered a cave to spend the night and received a fresh revelation of God. There he was strengthened and became a new man. The cave was not his tomb; it was a womb. He entered it with fear, but came out with new boldness. He had learned to lean on God. Jezebel's threat had not changed, but Elijah had changed. It was not his strength he was trying to lean on anymore; it was the divine strength of God that he was leaning on (see 1 Kings 19). I love to make this statement: "The longer you walk, the stronger you become; the longer you pray, the smaller you become." As God fills us with His power, we can accomplish the impossible. Like the apostle Paul, you and I can lean on God and declare, "I can do all things through Him who strengthens me" (Philippians 4:13 NASB).

Listen to the voice of God. God chose little Samuel, who helped Eli the priest in the Tabernacle, for great things. The small boy heard the audible voice of God calling him by name, and that call changed his life (see 1 Samuel 3:10). He grew up to be a priest, prophet and judge over the land of Israel. Let's learn to listen to the voice of God and follow it so that, like Samuel, we can live out the great plans God has laid out for our lives. As the prophet Isaiah said, "Whether you turn to the right or to the left, your ears will hear a voice behind you, saying, 'This is the way; walk in it'" (Isaiah 30:21).

Lead from darkness to light. Moses was the leader whom God chose to lead the vast number of Israelites from bondage to freedom, from Egypt to the Promised Land. Moses faced many challenges along the way—many of the Israelites murmured, many rebelled and many armies came against them. But he heard and obeyed the voice of God, leaned on God's strength and led the people through the wilderness. Jesus appointed the apostle Paul to carry the Gospel to the Gentiles, saying, "I am sending you to them to open their eyes and turn them from darkness to light, and from the power of Satan to God, so that they may receive forgiveness of sins and a place among those who are sanctified by faith in me" (Acts 26:17–18). Paul faced many challenges along the way, too, but like Moses, he let nothing distract him from the plan of God.

Let's resolve to live a life that is a beacon of hope to those who are lost and in search of God's love. Let's take the Light of the world to those suffering in darkness and show them the way. May we desire that God will enable us to work for His glory, knowing that our ultimate reward comes from Him. Let's learn to lean on our Master, knowing that He will be our shelter as we rest secure in Him. Let's be sensitive to hearing His voice, and let's be instruments in His hands to lead people to the saving knowledge of Christ.

Let's Pray Together

Loving heavenly Father, surround us with Your mighty presence. You are our comfort and our resting place. As Moses said of the Benjamites, let us be Your beloved who rest secure in You, because You are our shield and shelter.

Show us the places You want us to be, and allow us to meet the people You want us to meet. Help us be diligent in doing Your will. As we walk with You, we will not seek personal gain or the attention of others. We will lean on You and on Your understanding, not our own. We will listen for Your guiding voice to give us wisdom and direction in every situation.

Help us be a beacon of light in dark places, and help us lead people to Your love and redemption.

In Jesus' name we pray, Amen.

Afterword

Thriving in the Blessings of God

When we look at the beginnings of Jacob and his sons, it fills us with awe at the way God works in the lives of His children, fulfilling His plans. For a long while, Jacob appeared like a man whose life was controlled by his emotions and feelings, a man who never gave God a chance to work in his life. A deceiver, he just kept running away from God for over twenty years, till God met him and touched him. Then Jacob started experiencing real struggles—shame over the defilement of his only daughter, Dinah, and the pain of losing his son Joseph, whom he greatly loved. These struggles eventually brought changes in Jacob's life, causing him to come closer to God and build a relationship with Him. This ultimately opened his spiritual eyes to see and declare the future that God had in store for each of his sons individually.

It does not matter how you started your life. If you decide to connect with God, He can take your life and turn it around. He can make it fruitful, even to the extent of you becoming a prophet.

Tracing the life of each of Jacob's sons and the tribes that were named after them, it is amazing to see how, although their lives were painted differently, when put together they formed a beautiful rainbow. Jacob and Moses pronounced more than just material blessings on these men and their tribes; they went on to describe the spiritual blessings on them and the rich legacy they would leave behind. The accuracy of their prophecies is remarkable. Like an architect drawing a master plan of a building and then seeing the building rise before his very eyes, we can read the prophecies and see how accurately they came to pass even many years later.

The sons of Jacob were far from perfect; they were ordinary men who struggled with sin, struggled in their relationship with God and even struggled with people. Think of them—they were the very ones who planned to do away with their younger brother Joseph. Yet how much they changed, eventually protecting their youngest brother, Benjamin, with their very lives.

The twelve tribes of Israel remind me of the twelve disciples of Jesus Christ—imperfect, weak, confused and fearful men. Looking at these men, many would not have expected much from them. Yet God takes them and does great and powerful things through their lives! God is indeed silently working in everyone's life to fulfill His purposes.

Working on this book, studying the lives of Jacob's sons and the tribes that followed, and recollecting events in my own life and ministry, I have drawn closer to God. I am convinced that I should not take my relationship with God lightly. God is powerful and cannot be limited. He can do anything through my life, without looking at who I am or what I have done. This motivates me to spend more time reading the Word of God and learning to understand the immeasurable love of God that is at work in my life. I look at my life and marvel at how I started from day one with nothing in my hand except an unwavering trust in God. Constantly seeking His face and strongly trusting in His promises has affirmed my calling. I am confident that as I keep trusting Him, He will enable me to take the church to the next level. This study of each tribe and their blessings has made me thrive in God, and I trust that it has done the same for you.

God has not forgotten you. Be confident that God has amazing things planned for you. The apostle Paul declared, "As it is written: 'No eye has seen, no ear has heard, no mind has conceived what God has prepared for those who love him'" (1 Corinthians 2:9 NIV1984).

You might say, "But I don't see anything happening." Build your relationship with God, and He will open your spiritual eyes to see His marvelous work in your life. The blessings God has pronounced over your life cannot be revoked. They will be fulfilled in every detail accurately. May you increase in the knowledge of God and experience every one of the blessings we have discovered in these pages, along with many more that God has for you.

Paul Thangiah preached his first sermon at the age of fifteen. Profoundly influenced by the life and ministry of his parents, he went on to become the founder and senior pastor of Full Gospel Assembly of God Church (FGAG) in Bangalore, Karnataka, India, with a congregation of over 25,000 people. He says that his heart's desire is to see India washed by the blood of the Lamb, and he often tells God, *Give me no name; give me no fame. Give me souls for India to be saved!*

Pastor Paul has traveled to more than 64 nations to lead "Prayer Penetration" ministries and to encourage pastors and church leadership. His television broadcast, *This Is Your Miracle*, reaches millions of homes in India and other nations. Pastor Paul also serves as superintendent of the Central District of the South India Assemblies of God, comprising the states of Karnataka and Goa and consisting of more than 1,000 churches.

Pastor Paul and his wife, Sheba, have been married for over thirty years. She has been beside him in ministry every step of the way, and together they have learned the importance of having Jesus at the very center of a marriage. Sheba currently oversees the counseling department at FGAG and is pursuing her doctorate in ministry, with a concentration in pastoral counseling.

Pastor Paul and Sheba have two children, Grace Catherine and Roger Samuel. Grace serves as her father's invaluable personal assistant and special events coordinator, while her husband, Neal, applies his creative talents in FGAG's media department and plays a vital role in strategically planning for the development and expansion of the church. Grace and Neal, with great joy, are expecting the arrival of their first child. Roger Samuel and his wife, Nicole, head the missions department of FGAG and pastor the church's New Generation service, with more than eight hundred young people coming every Sunday. They have also given Pastor Paul two wonderful grandsons, Malachi James and Josiah Paul.

For more information on Pastor Paul's ministry and materials, visit FGAG online at www.fgag.in and www.fgag.tv, or find him at www.facebook.com/RevPaulThangiah.